Illustrator
Ken Tunell

Editor
Mara Ellen Guckian

Editorial Project Manager
Ina Massler Levin, M.A.

Editor-in-Chief
Sharon Coan, M.S. Ed.

Creative Director
Elayne Roberts

Art Coordinator
Denice Adorno

Cover Artist
Denise Bauer

Product Manager
Phil Garcia

Imaging
Ralph Olmedo, Jr.
Rosa C. See

Publishers
Rachelle Cracchiolo, M.S. Ed.
Mary Dupuy Smith, M.S. Ed.

Big & Easy Patterns

Holidays • School Days • Seasons • Themes

Compiled by

Loralyn Radcliffe

Teacher Created Materials, Inc.
6421 Industry Way
Westminster, CA 92683
www.teachercreated.com
©2004 Teacher Created Materials, Inc.
Made in U.S.A.
ISBN-0-7439-3801-1

Table of Contents

Table of Contents

Using the Patterns

There are several ways to use the patterns in this book. The pieces are big and easy to cut out and assemble. They can be used by students as well as teachers. Reduce or enlarge them to fit your needs. Try to laminate pieces you will be placing in your centers.

Color-and-Cut Figures and Paper Sculpture

For an easy-to-prepare art project, simply reproduce the patterns on white construction paper, and have children color, cut out, and glue the pieces together at the tabs so that the finished product looks like the diagram. If the pattern would benefit from moving parts, try using brads instead of glue.

To make a stuffed paper sculpture, trace the outline of the assembled figure onto another blank piece of paper, decorate it, and cut it out. Put the two pieces together and staple them around the edges leaving one side open. Lightly stuff with crumpled newspaper, and then staple the opening shut.

Classroom Decorations and Story Prompts

The patterns can be used on bulletin boards, flannel boards, or magnetic boards. Copy the patterns on heavy stock, assemble, and then laminate them. Glue squares of felt or Velcro® to the back for use on the flannelboard, or attach the magnetic strips available at craft stores for magnetic board use. You can also hang the patterns from the ceiling with fishing line or use them to create mobiles. Use the patterns to generate class discussions about the various seasons and holidays and to spark ideas for story and journal writing.

Word Banks

A word bank is a collection of related words that grows as students learn more about the specific topic. Children gain ownership of the word bank as they add more words to the list. You can create a word bank for the fall with a basket of apples. Winter words can be gathered on snowflakes swirling around a snowman. Write letters, math facts, etc., right on the pattern. Use adhesive labels or white out to conceal design elements.

Puppets and Paper Dolls

Give each child a copy of a pattern to color, cut out, and glue to a craft stick for his or her own stick puppet. For a teacher set, use cardstock and laminate before gluing. You may wish to reduce the patterns or use the diagrams of fully assembled figures and enlarge to meet your needs, or make larger puppets. Attach the yardsticks or paint stirrers from the hardware store instead of craft sticks. Place a set of the laminated, colored patterns without craft sticks in the Drama Center for the students' use. Encourage the children to create their own dramas, and to make new clothes and accessories for the figures.

Big Books and Shape Books

Many of the patterns in this book lend themselves well to big books. Patterns can be used as covers, or they can be decorations for the inside pages. To make a big book, cut two pieces of poster board to the desired size and glue the colored pattern to one of the pieces. Punch holes down the side and bind all pages with yarn or rings. You can also make a large shape book by copying the pattern onto two pieces of cardstock for the front and back. Trim lined paper to fit inside the covers and bind the book with yarn, rings, or staples. Big books and shape books can be used for class-generated stories, poems, investigations, or reports, or they can be used as journals.

Scarecrow

Use pages 5–7. Cut out and color all pieces. Connect the head to torso at Tab A. Connect the arms to torso at Tabs B & C. Connect the scarecrow feet to torso at Tabs D & E.

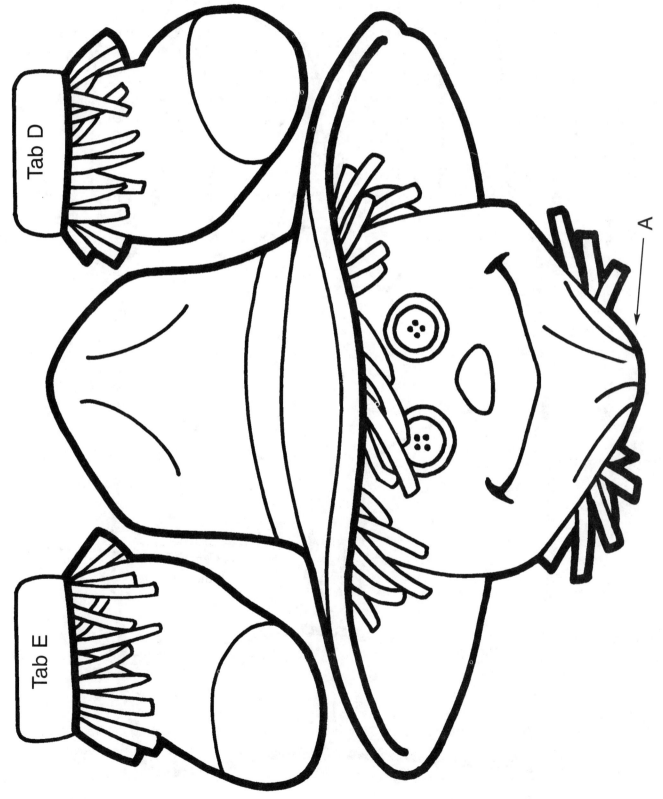

Scarecrow *(cont.)*

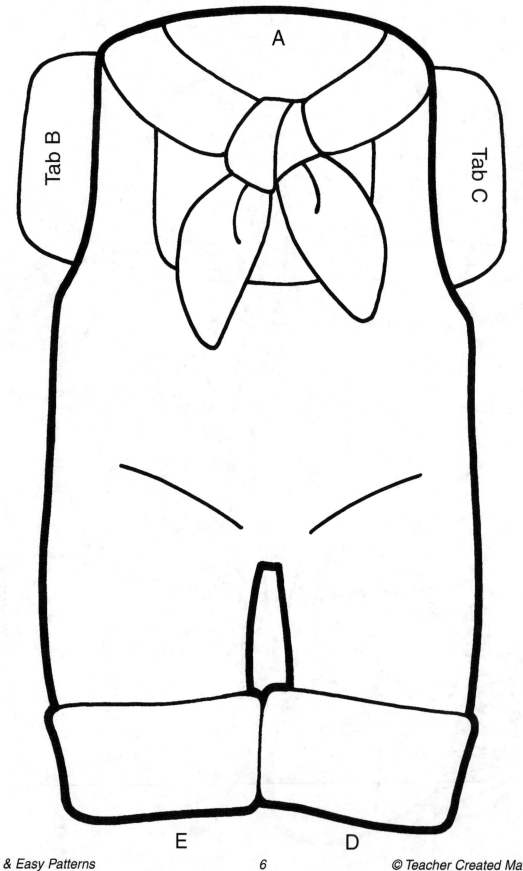

Scarecrow *(cont.)*

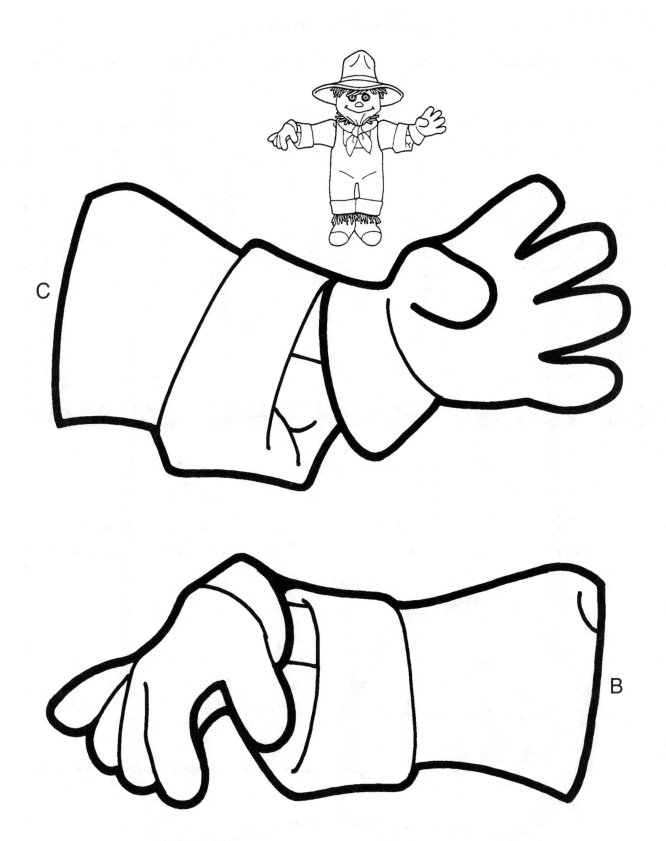

C

B

School Bus

Use pages 8–9. Connect the bus at the tab.

Autumn Leaves *(cont.)*

Oak

Autumn Leaves *(cont.)*

Poplar

Squirrel

Use pages 13–15. See page 14 for directions.

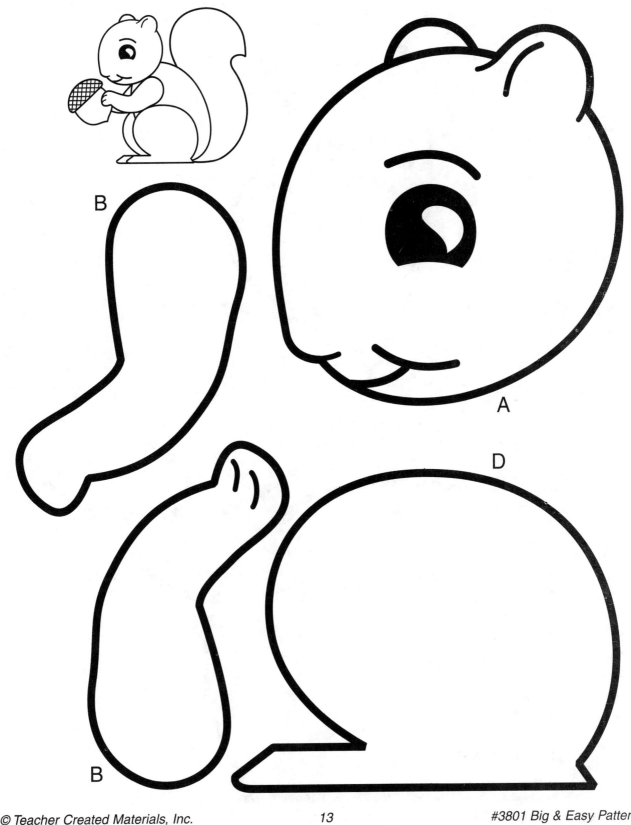

B

A

D

B

Squirrel *(cont.)*

Attach squirrel head to A.
Attach arms to either side
of paper at B.
Place acorn between
paws. Attach legs to
either side
of paper at D.
Attach the tail at C.

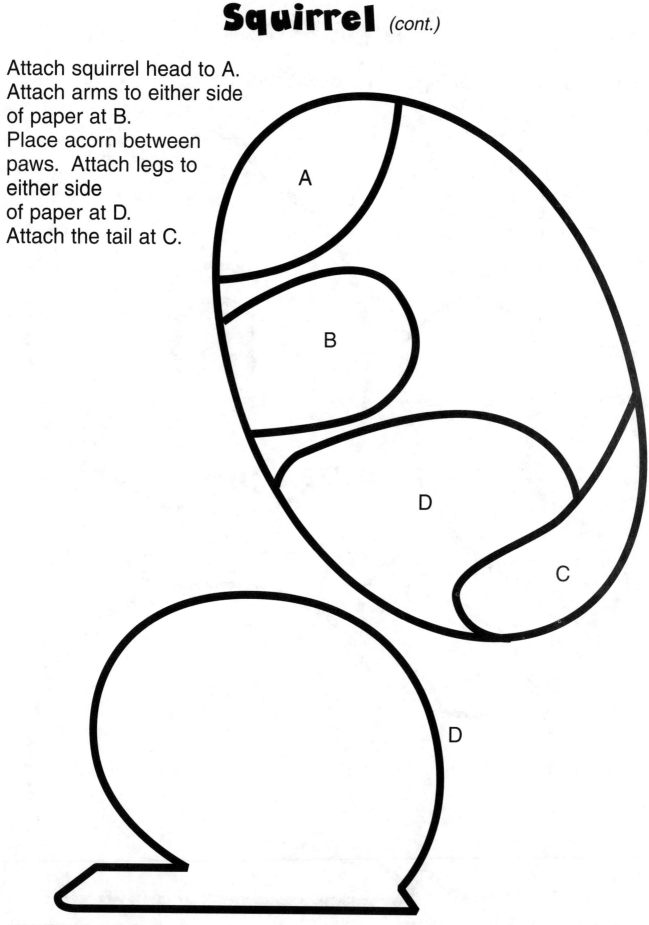

14

Squirrel *(cont.)*

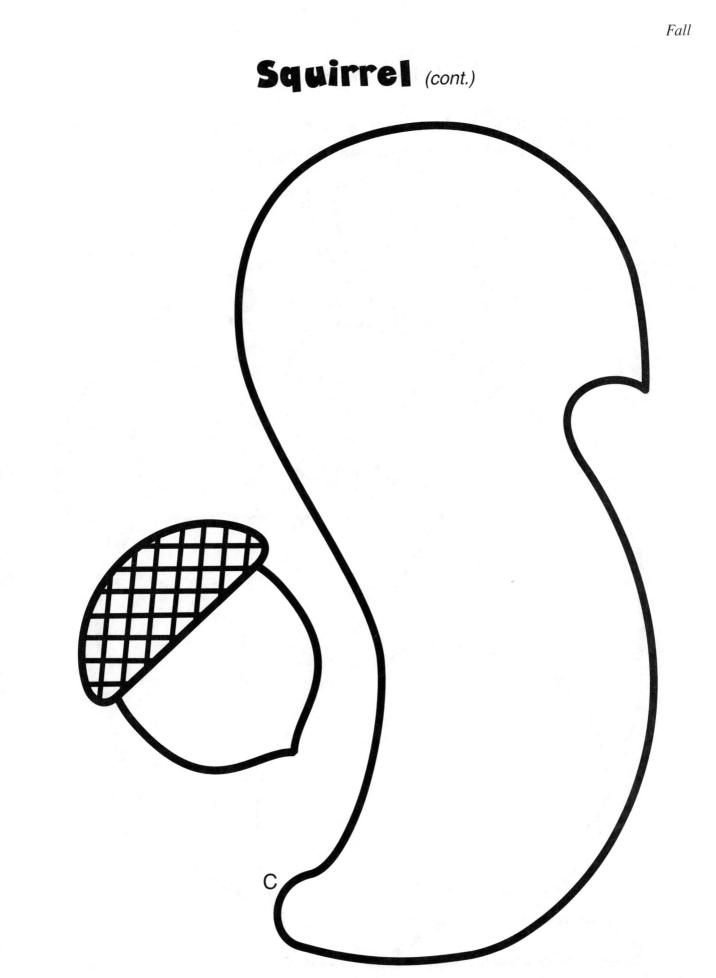

C

Acorn

Add lines to create fall stationery or enlarge to use as a journal cover. Duplicate pattern to create a word wall.

16

Basket

Use pages 17–18. Cut out and color pieces. Connect the basket at the tab. Cut on the dotted line to open basket.

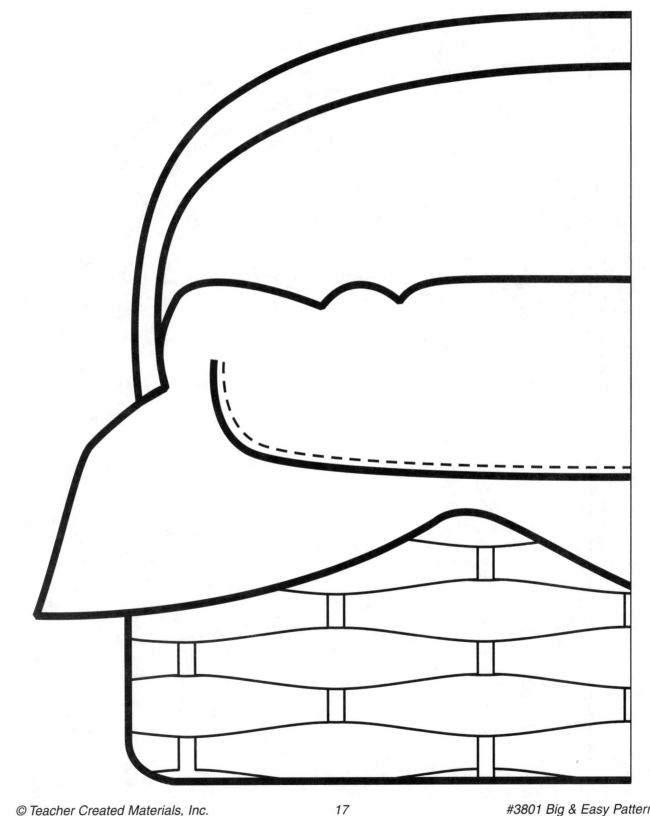

Basket *(cont.)*

Fill the basket with autumn leaves (pages 10–12), acorns (page 15), apples (page 19), or vegetables and fruits (pages 54–55).

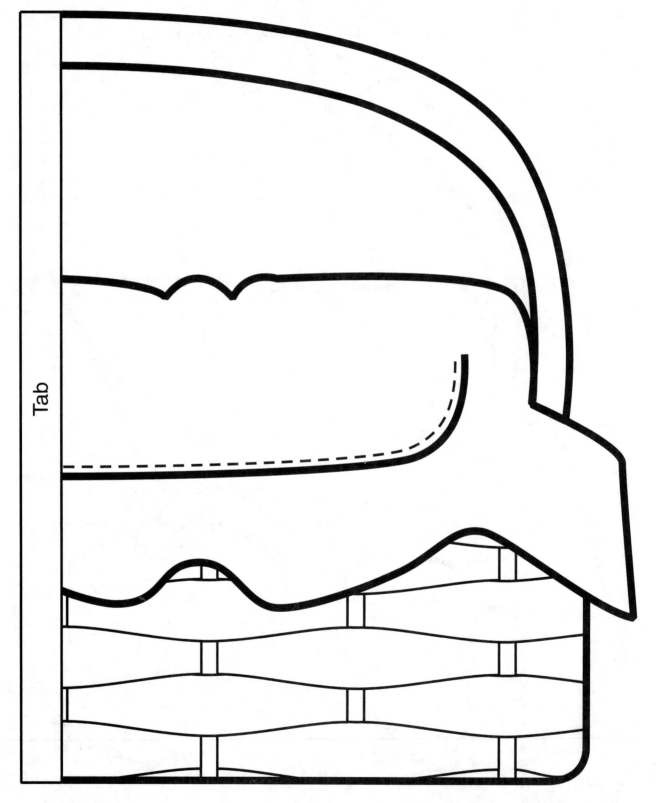

Christopher Columbus

Use pages 23–25. Attach the head to torso at Tab A. Attach the arm to torso at Tab B and legs to torso at Tab C.

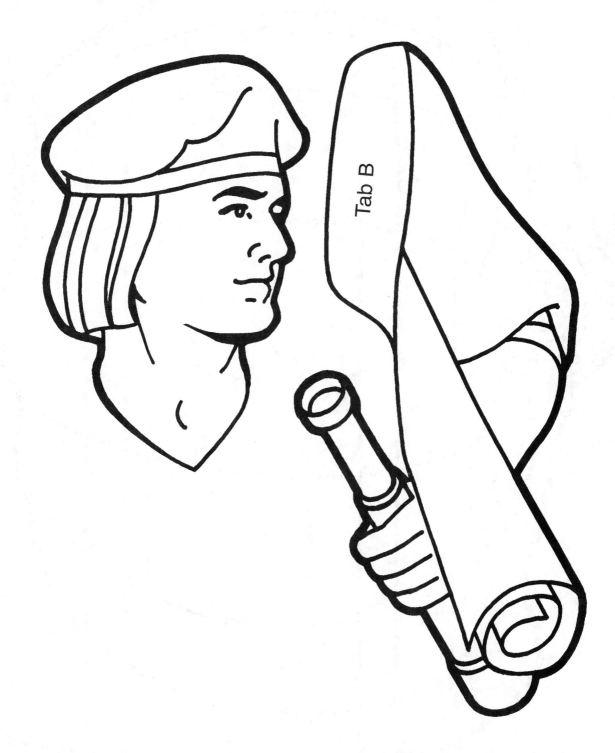

Christopher Columbus *(cont.)*

Cat

Bat

34

Skeleton

Use pages 35–37. Attach the skull to Tab A. Connect the upper and lower arms to Tabs C & D. Attach the left arm to Tab B and the right arm to Tab E. Connect the upper and lower legs to Tabs H & I. Attach the left leg to Tab F and right leg to Tab G. Use brads instead of glue or tape if you want the skeleton to move.

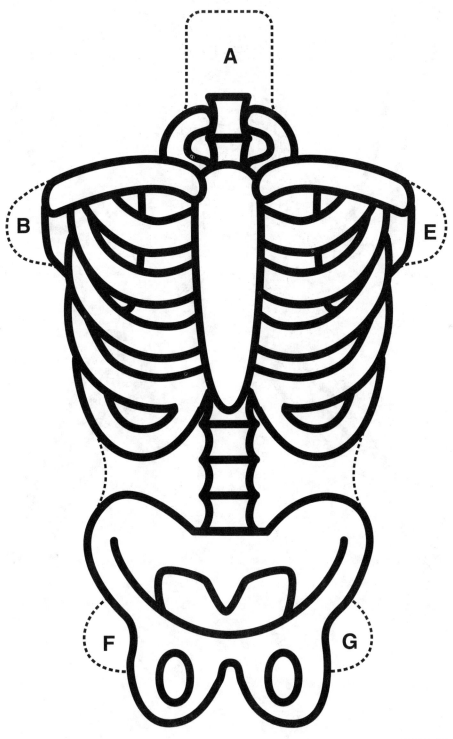

Skeleton *(cont.)*

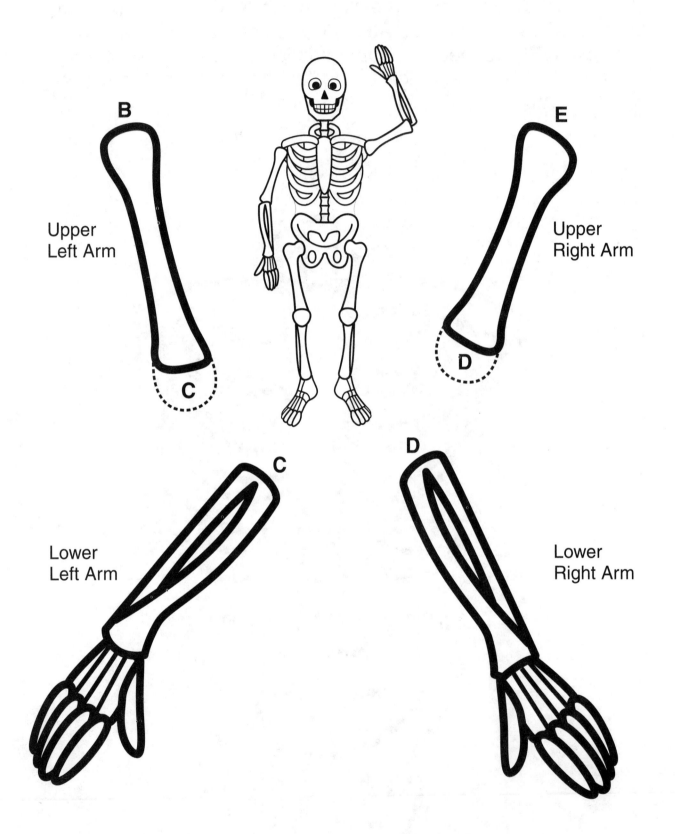

B

Upper
Left Arm

C

E

Upper
Right Arm

D

C

Lower
Left Arm

D

Lower
Right Arm

Skeleton *(cont.)*

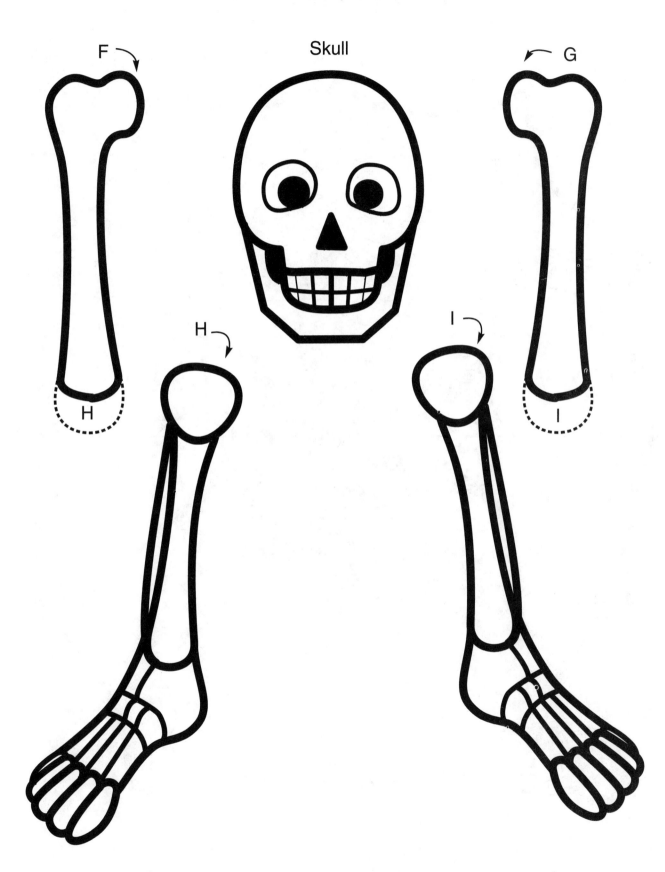

F

Skull

G

H

I

H

I

Spider and Web

Pilgrim Boy

Use pages 39–41. Attach the head to torso at Tab A. Overlap torso on legs at C and the left arm to the torso at B. This pattern was designed to work with, or without, the rifle. Determine if you wish to use the rifle. If so, do not glue the right arm down completely. Instead, attach only at shoulder at D.

D

A

Pilgrim Boy *(cont.)*

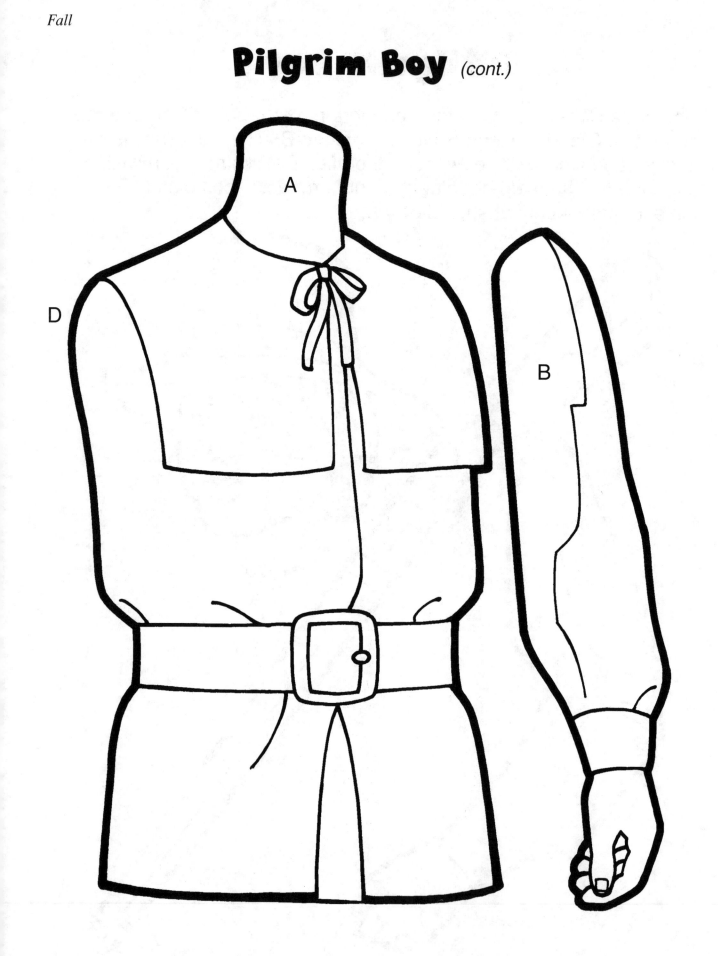

Pilgrim Boy *(cont.)*

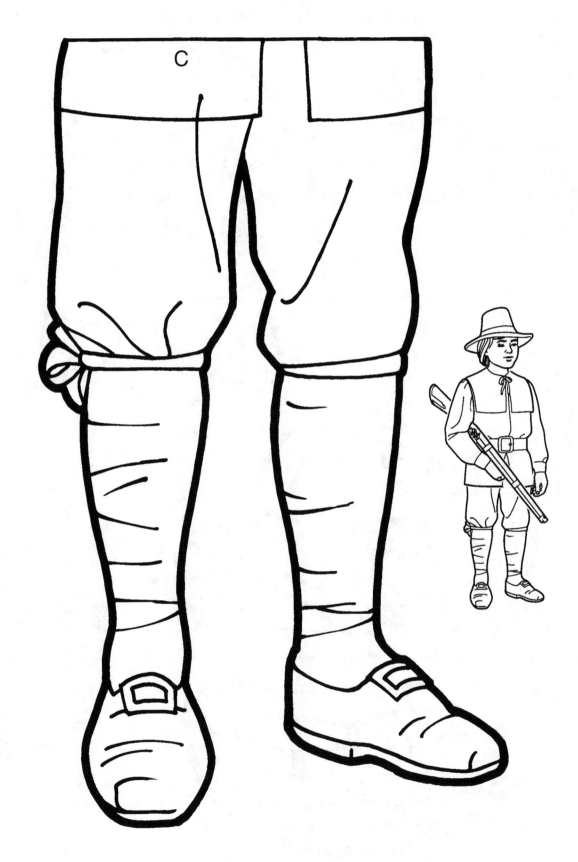

Pilgrim Girl

Use pages 42–44. Attach the head to the torso at Tab A. Attach the legs to the torso at Tab B.

This pattern was designed to work with, or without the basket.
If you wish to use the basket, cut around the right hand and the basket handle.
Then slide the basket on.

Pilgrim Girl *(cont.)*

A

Pilgrim Girl *(cont.)*

Tab B

Native American Girl

Use pages 45–47. Attach the head to torso at Tab A and legs to torso at tab B. Place vegetables in girl's left arm.

Native American Girl *(cont.)*

46

Native American Girl *(cont.)*

Tab B

Native American Boy

Use pages 48–50. Attach the head to torso at Tab A and legs to torso at Tab B. The pattern was created to make use of the bow and arrow optional. If you choose to include it, carefully cut around hand and slip bow and arrow underneath.

Native American Boy *(cont.)*

Native American Boy *(cont.)*

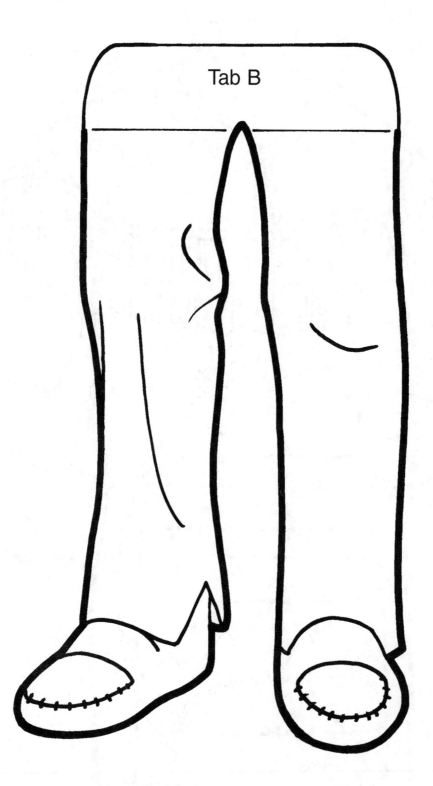

Tab B

Mayflower

Add this sail to the ship on pages 26–28.

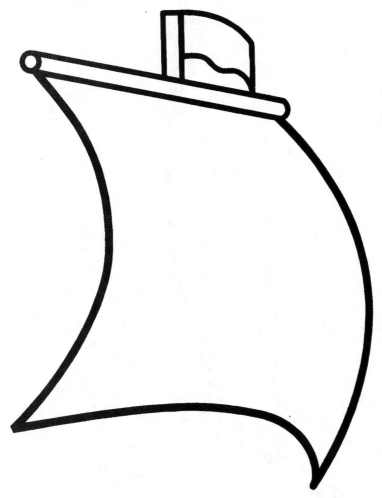

Cornucopia

Use pages 52–53. Color, cut out, then glue the cornucopia together at the tab. Make a slit on the dotted line to slip in fruits and vegetables. Use reduced copies of the apple (page 19), the pumpkin (page 22), and the acorn (page 15) in addition to the vegetables and fruits (pages 54–55).

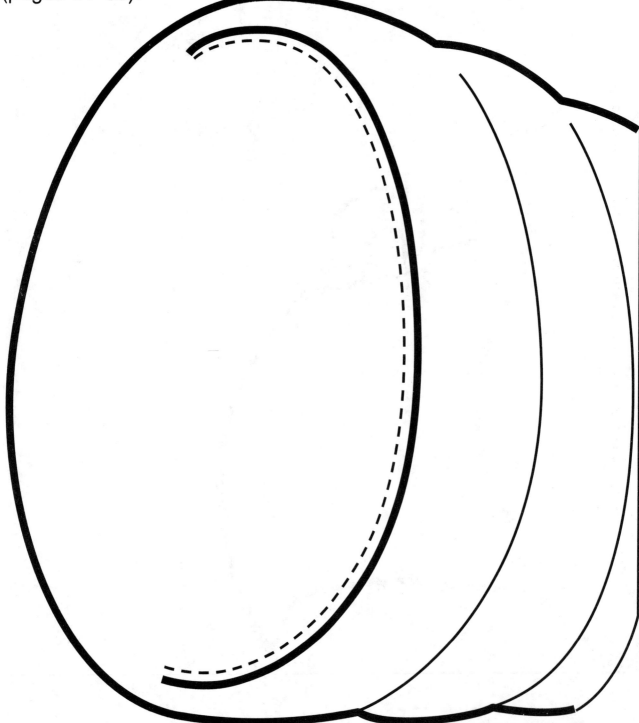

Cornucopia *(cont.)*

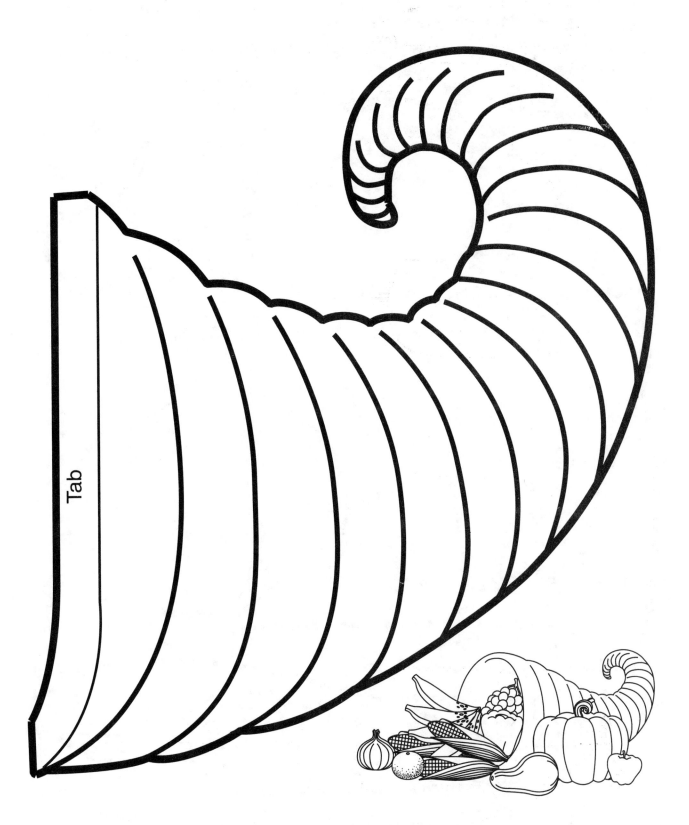

Tab

Vegetables

54

Fruits

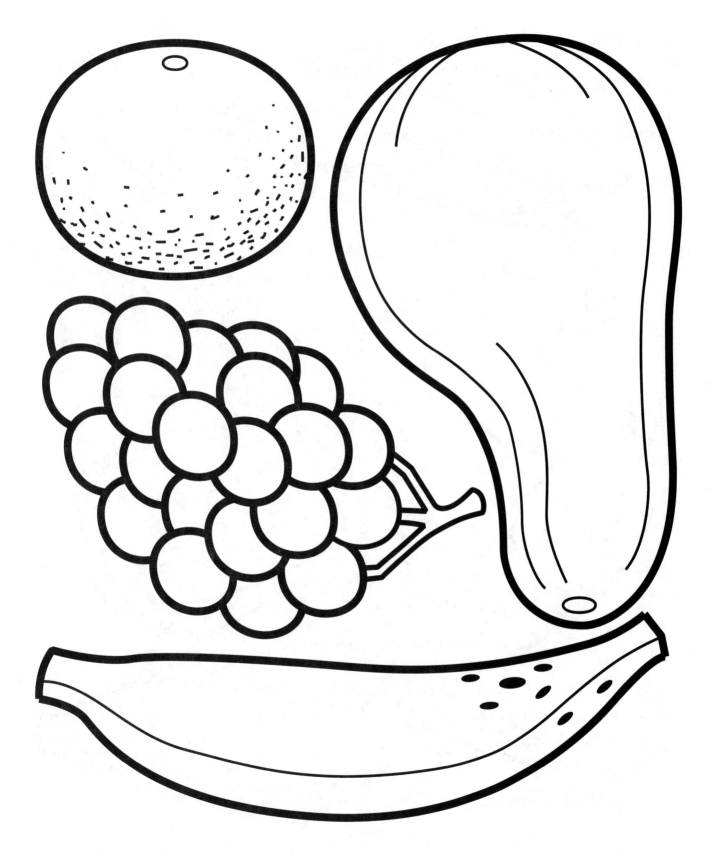

Turkey

Turkey Feathers

White out interior lines to use for word walls, math facts, etc.

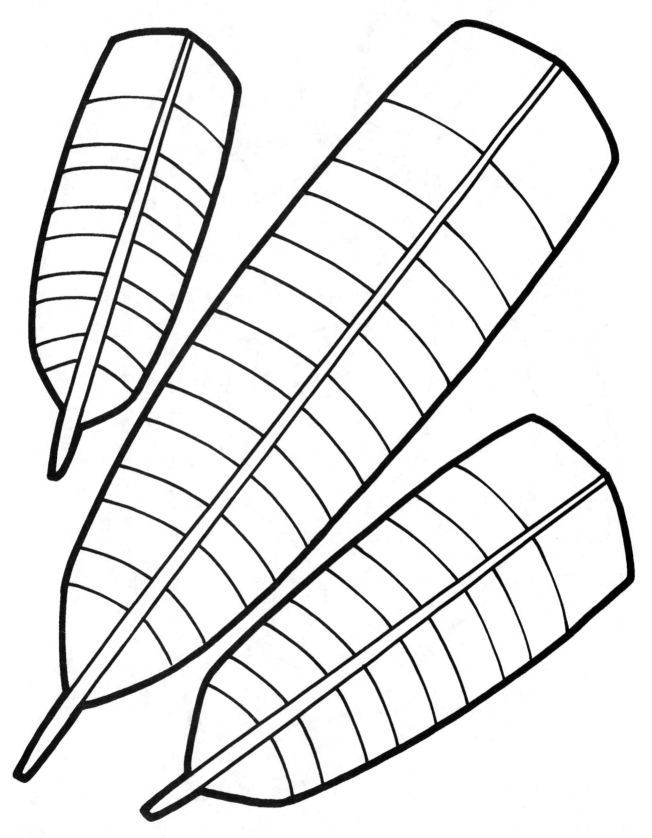

Turkey Dinner

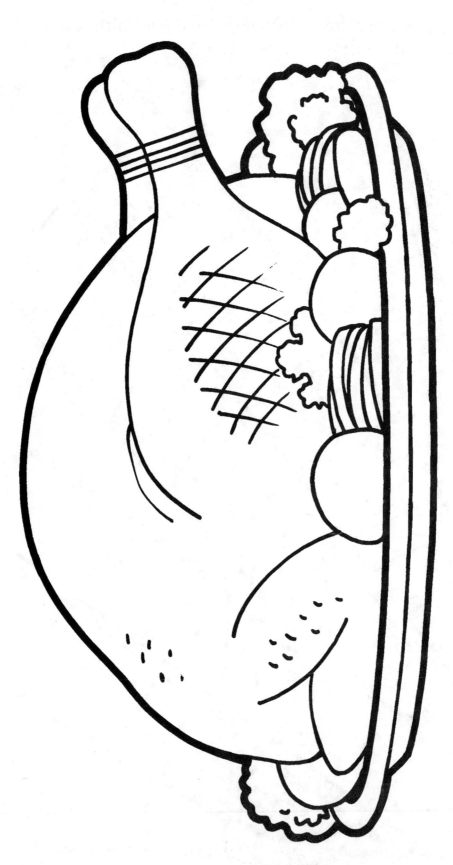

58

Mittens

Mittens can be used to create borders, word walls, etc. Try them on the snowman on page 65.

Polar Bear

Use pages 62–64. Attach the polar bear's head to the torso at Tab A. Attach the legs B, C, D, and E as marked. Attach the tail at Tab F.

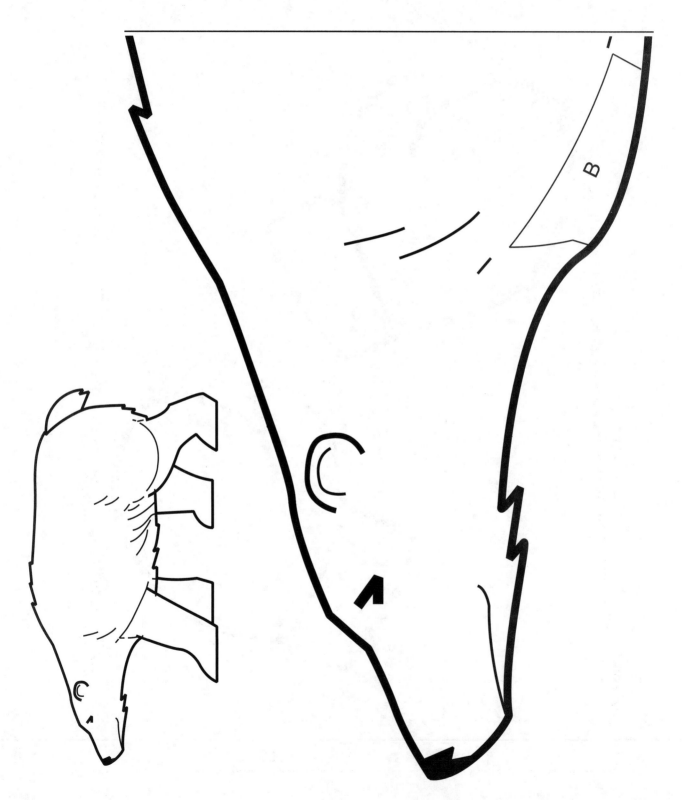

62

Polar Bear (cont.)

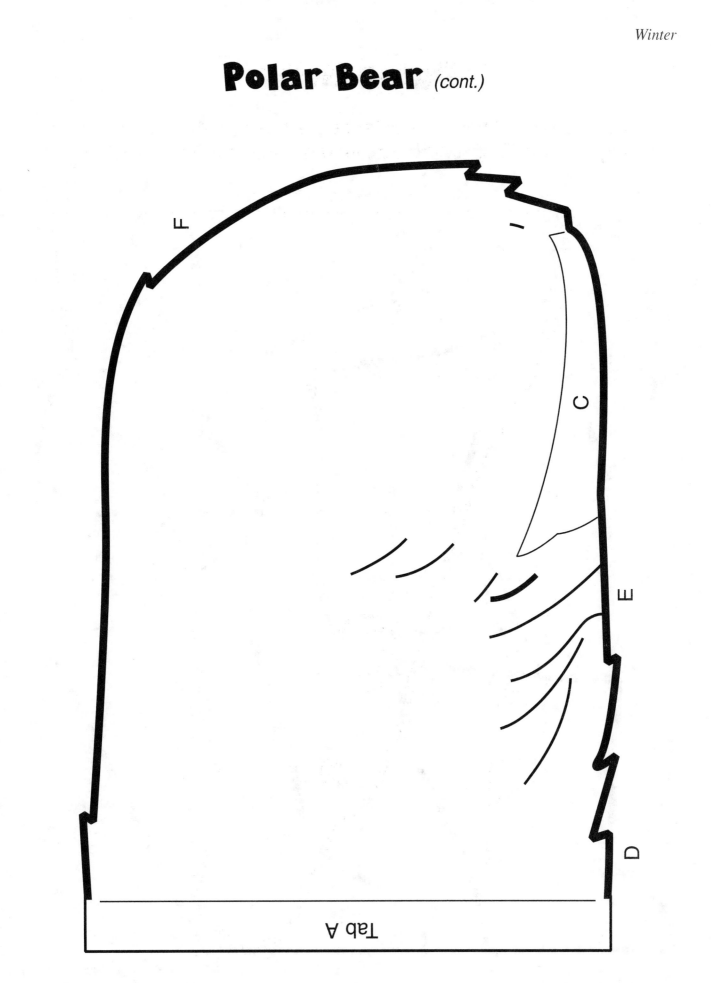

Polar Bear *(cont.)*

Snowman

Use pages 65–66. Try the snow cap on page 60 to decorate your snowman. You may also wish to use mittens (page 61) and boots (page 60) to dress your snowman. Attach the snowman head to the tab. Place branch arms where appropriate.

Snowman *(cont.)*

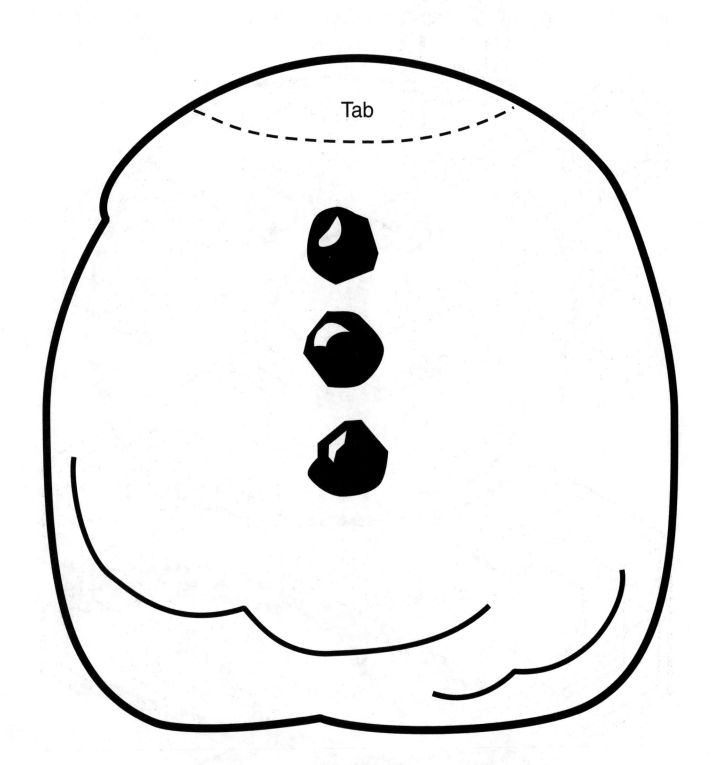

Snowflakes

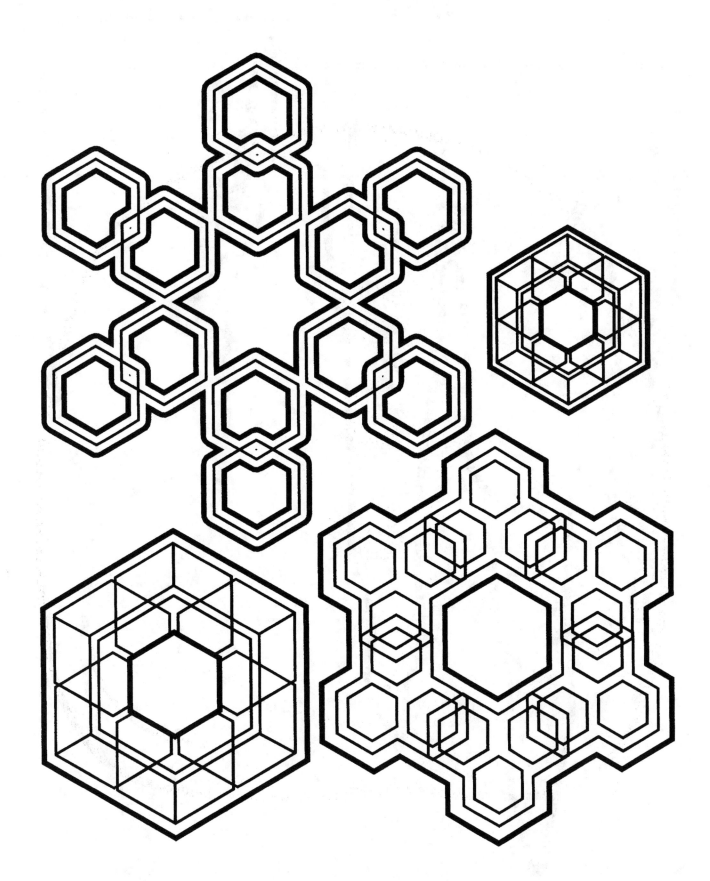

Icicles

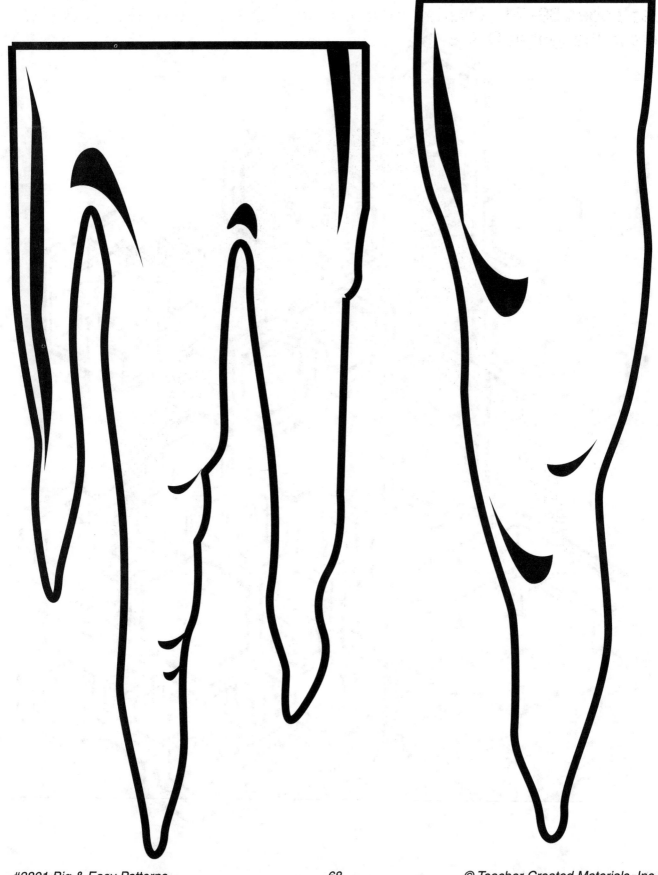

Penguin

Use pages 69–71. Overlap torso on tab A. Attach the wings at B & C.
Attach the feet at D & E.

Tab A

Cut here

Penguin *(cont.)*

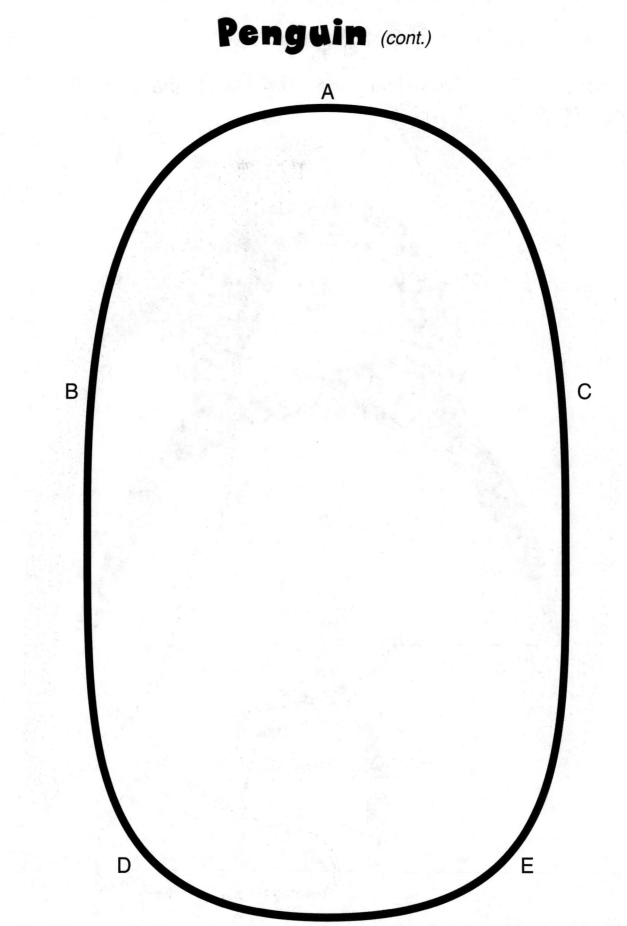

Penguin *(cont.)*

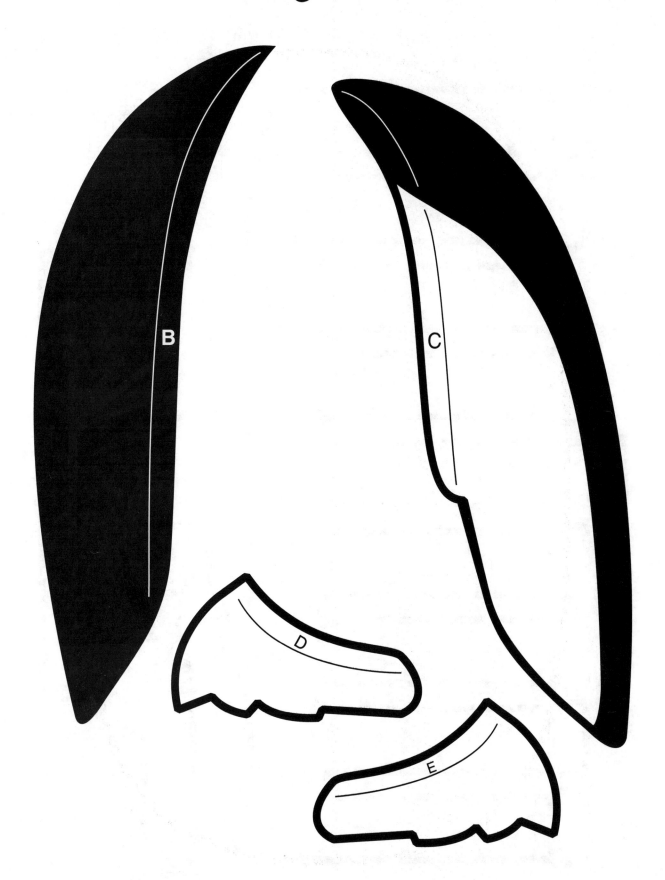

Menorah

Duplicate candle shown or make your own with strips of construction paper or wrapping paper.

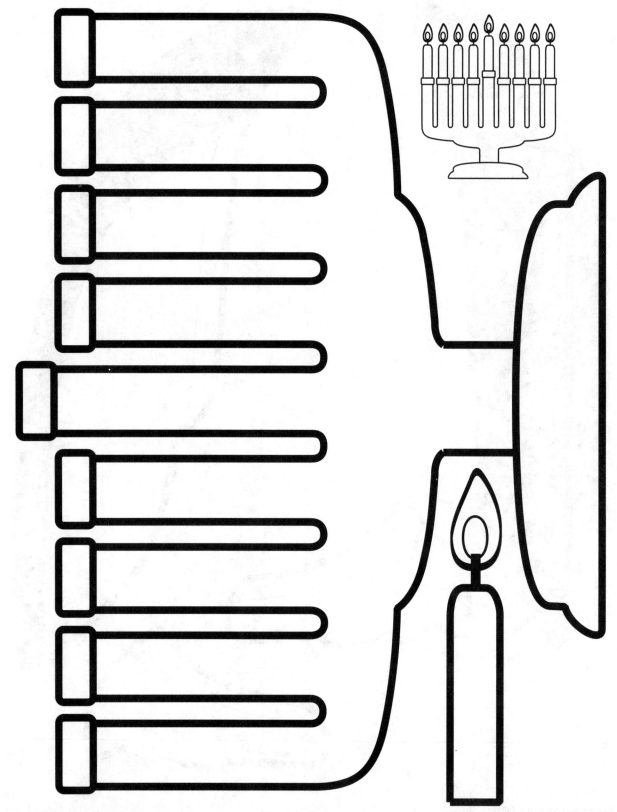

72

Dreidel

Dreidel *(cont.)*

74

Star of David

Santa Claus

Use pages 76–78. Overlap torso on pants at Tab A. Place bag of gifts below left mitten.

Santa Claus *(cont.)*

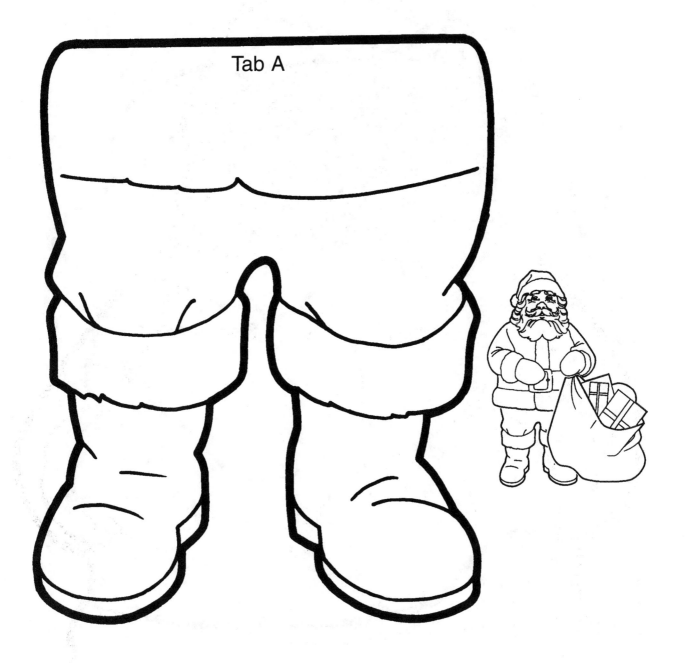

Tab A

Santa Claus *(cont.)*

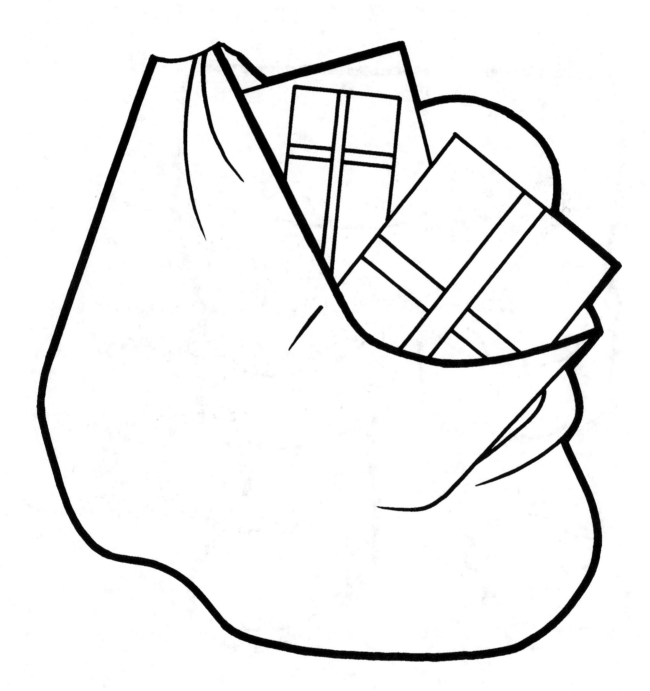

78

Reindeer

Use pages 79–81. Attach the reindeer's head to the torso at Tab A.
Connect the torso at Tab B.

A

Reindeer *(cont.)*

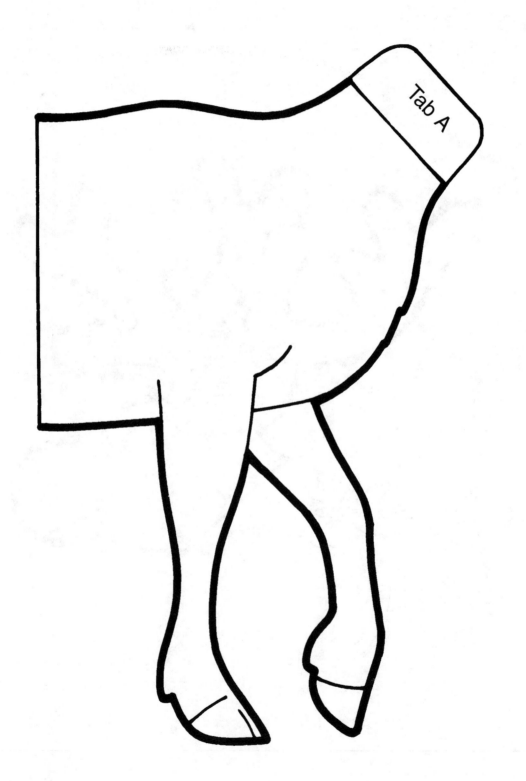

Tab A

80

Reindeer *(cont.)*

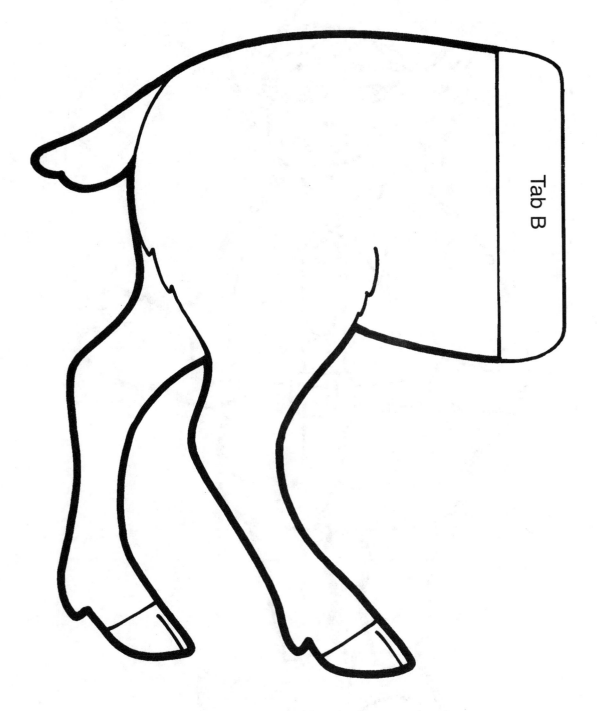

Tab B

Elf

Sitting Elf

The sitting elf was created to sit in the sleigh on pages 84–85.

Sleigh

Use pages 84–85. Connect the sleigh at the tab. Use with Santa, elves and reindeer on preceding pages.

Sleigh *(cont.)*

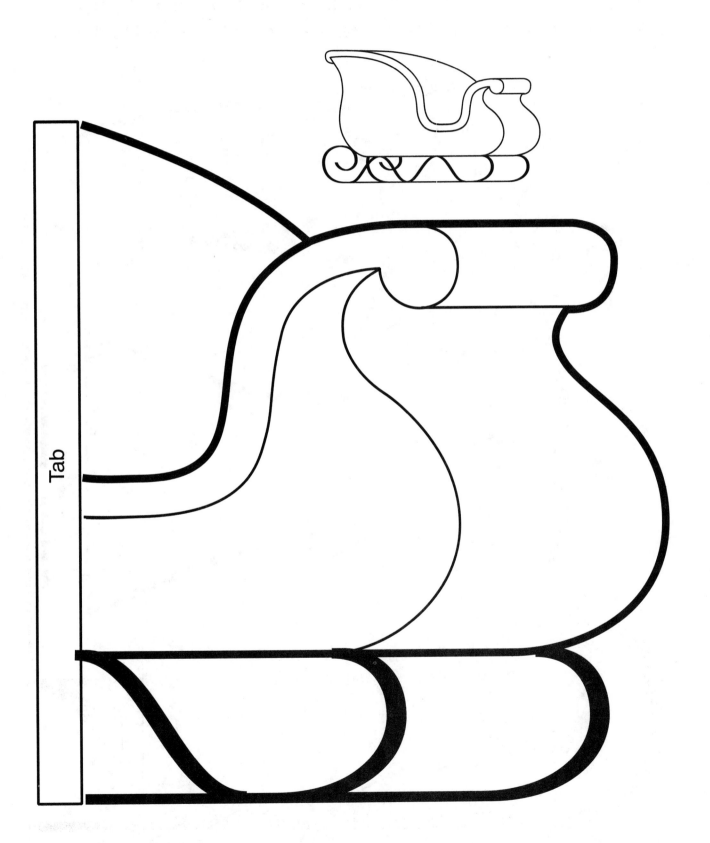

Tab

Christmas Tree

Use pages 86–88. Attach the top of tree to midsection at Tab A. Attach the midsection to base at Tab B. Place star on the top of the tree and decorate.

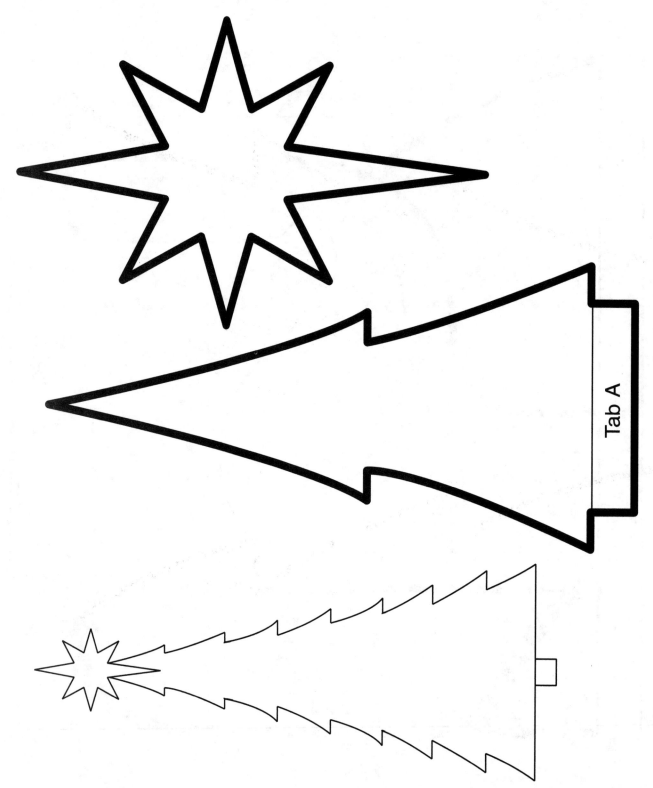

Tab A

86

Christmas Tree *(cont.)*

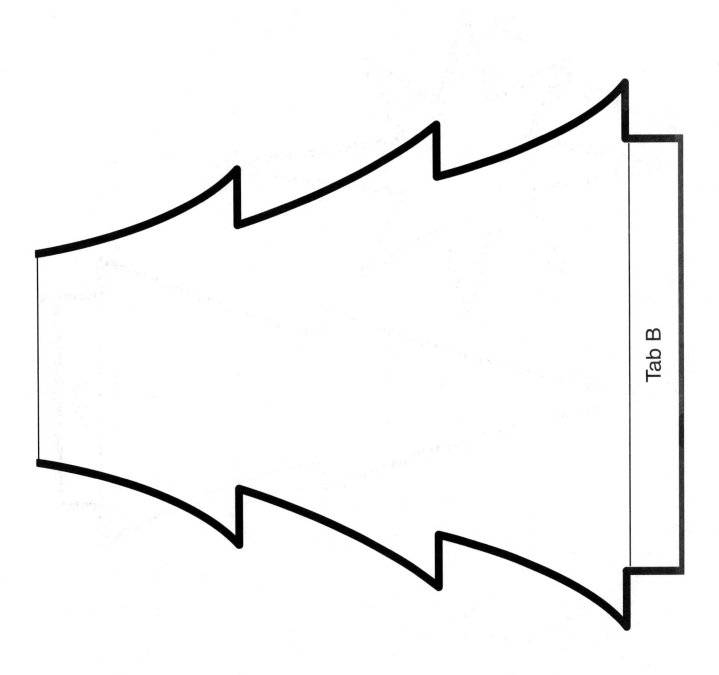

Tab B

Christmas Tree *(cont.)*

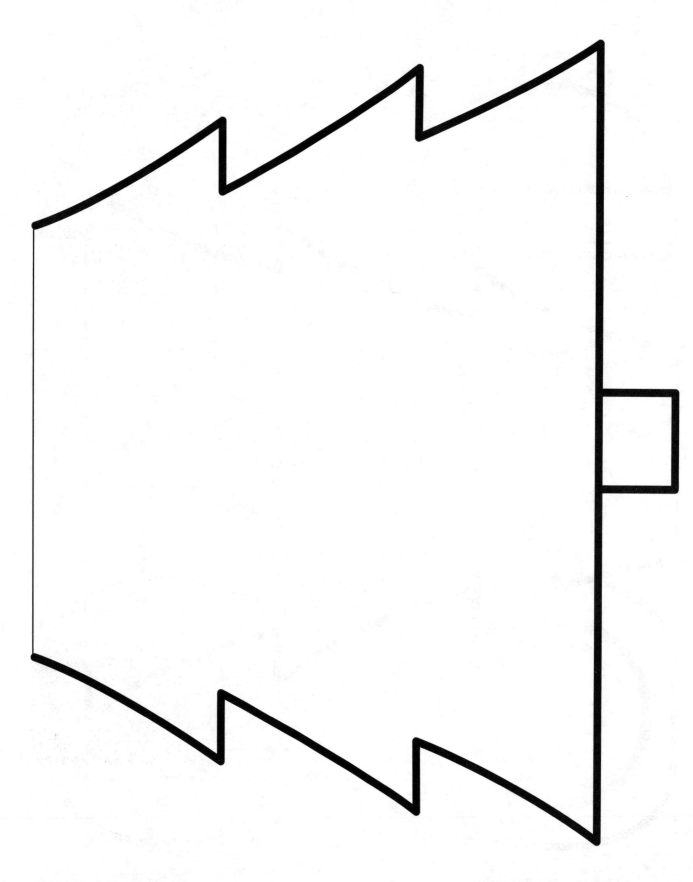

Ornaments

Gift

Stocking

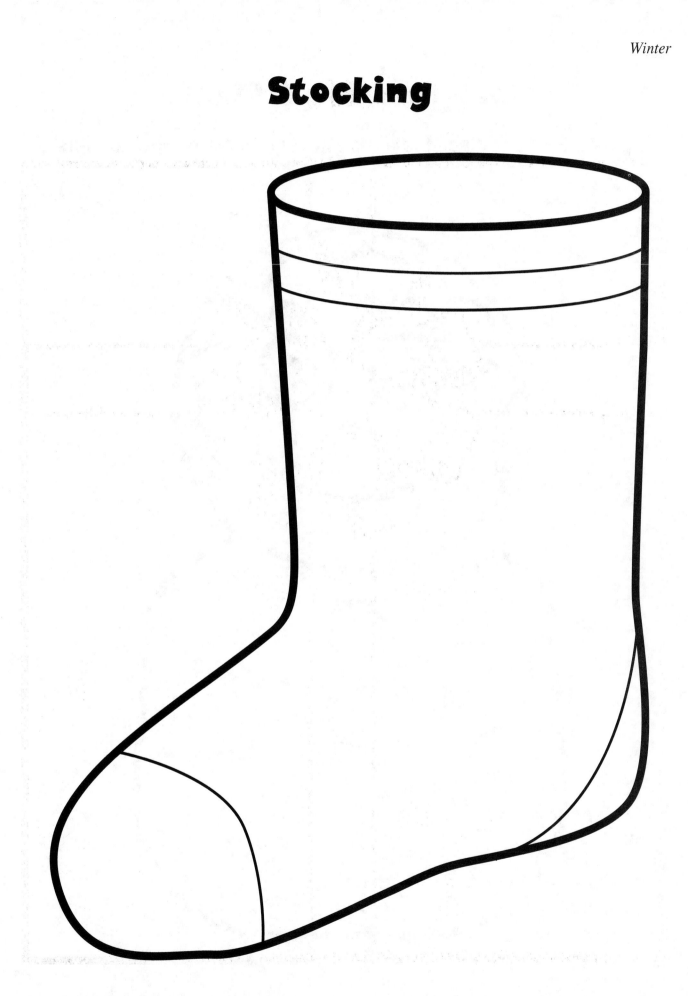

Gingerbread Man

Use pages 92–93. Attach the arms and legs to the back of the torso.

Arm

Arm

Leg

Leg

92

Gingerbread Man *(cont.)*

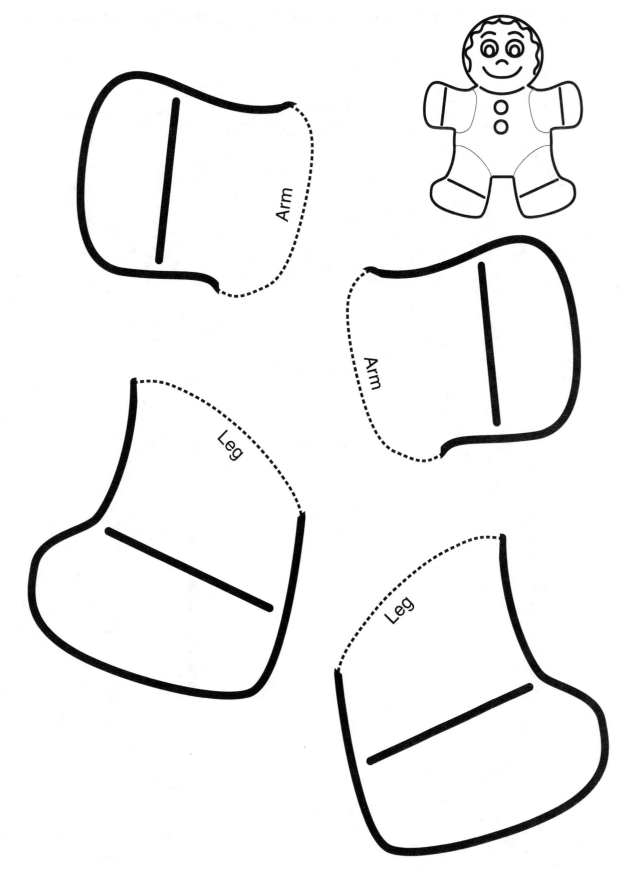

Arm

Arm

Leg

Leg

Candy Cane

Use pages 94–95. Connect the candy cane at the tab.

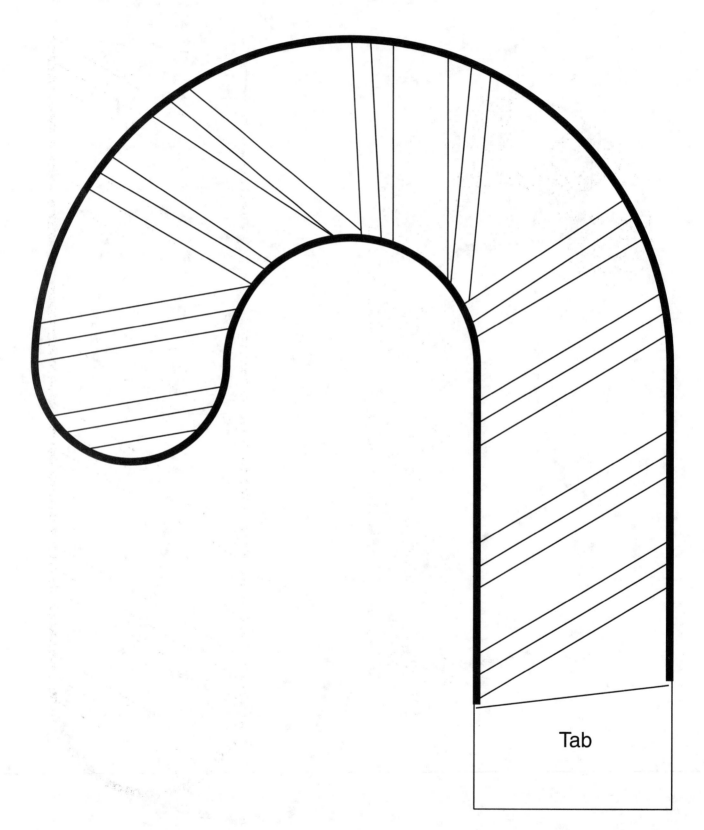

Tab

Candy Cane *(cont.)*

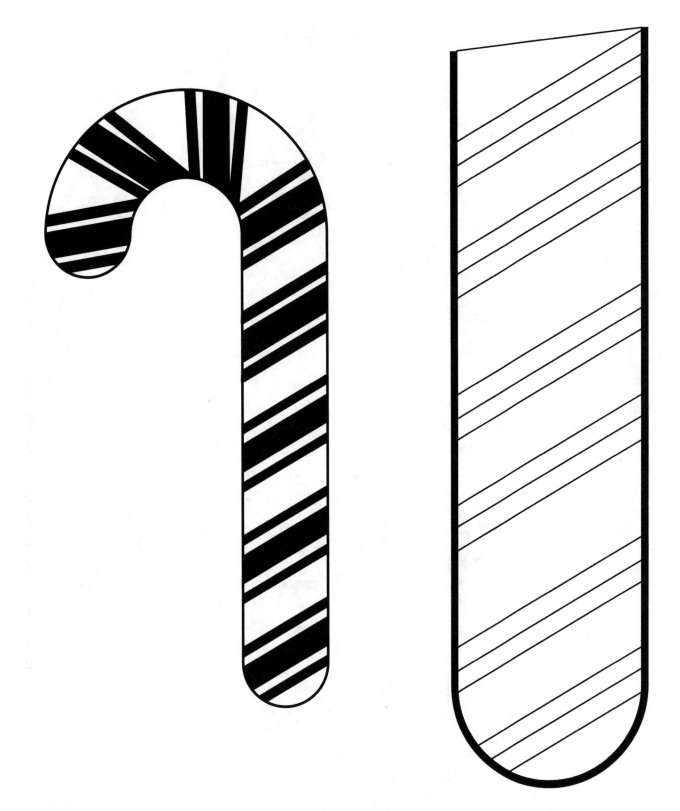

Wreath

Use pages 96–97. Connect the wreath at tabs.

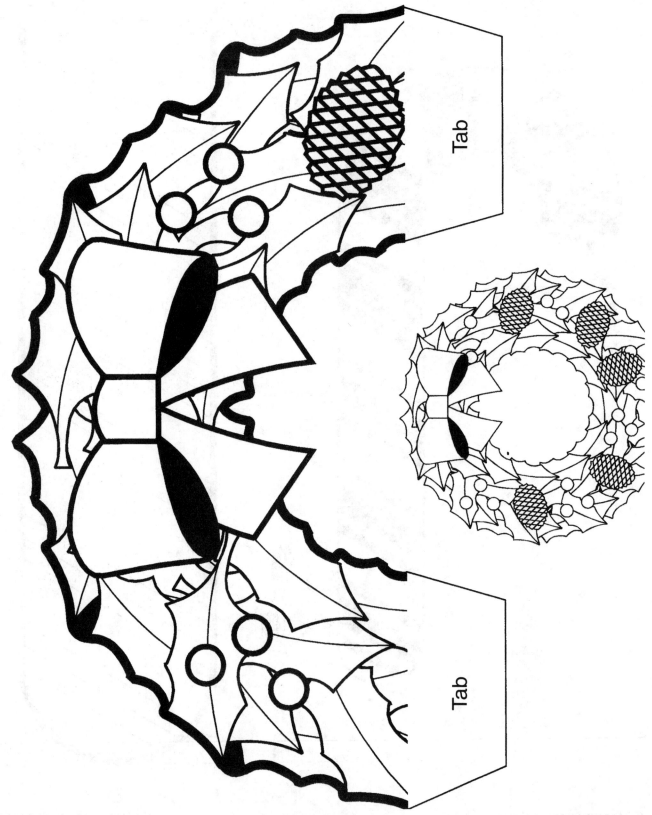

Wreath *(cont.)*

Holly

Mistletoe

Kinara

The kinara is a special candleholder with seven candles used during Kwanzaa. Three candles should be red and three should be green. The central candle is black.

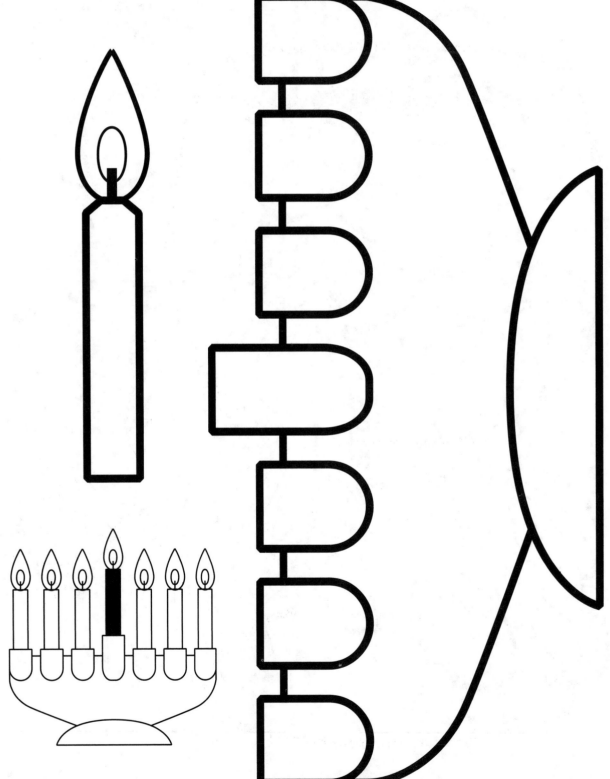

Kikombe

Use the kikombe (cup) in a Kwanzaa display and surround it with fruits (pages 19 & 55) and vegetables (page 54).

Mkeka

The mkeka is the first symbol of Kwanzaa. Traditionally, the mkeka is woven into interesting patterns. Have students create their own designs using crayons or markers.

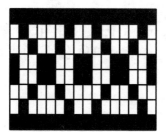

New Year's Party Hat

Martin Luther King, Jr.

Use pages 104–106. Attach the head to torso at Tab A. Connect the left arm to torso at Tab B and legs to torso at Tab C.

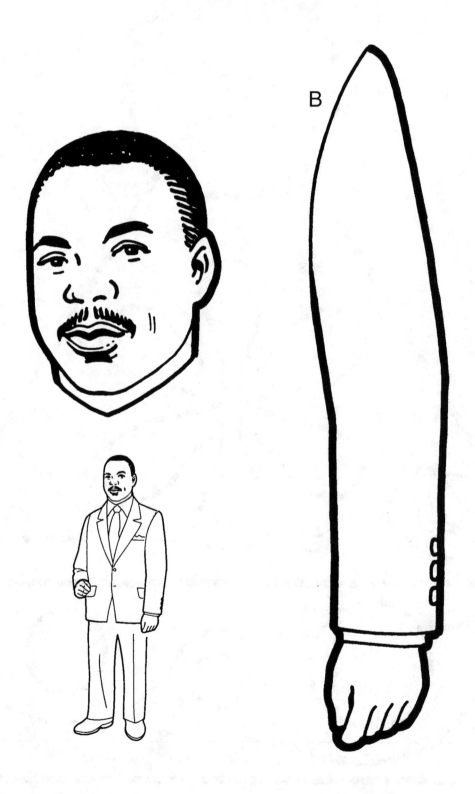

Martin Luther King, Jr. *(cont.)*

Martin Luther King, Jr. *(cont.)*

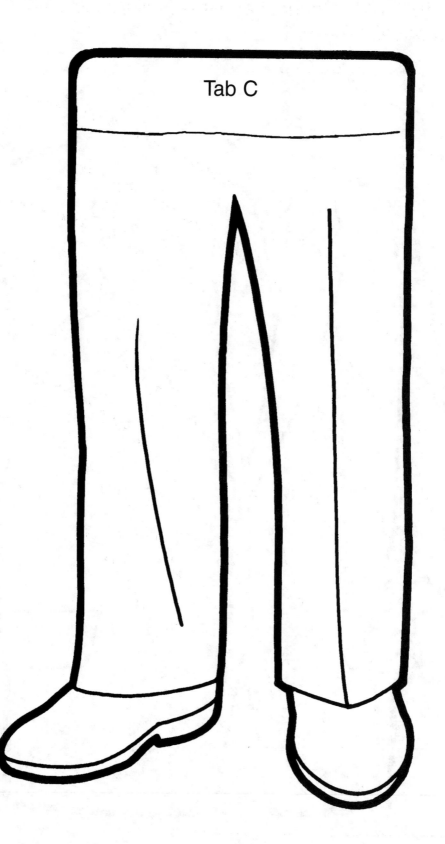

Tab C

Rainbow

Use pages 107–108. Connect at the tab. You may wish to add the clouds from pages 163–164.

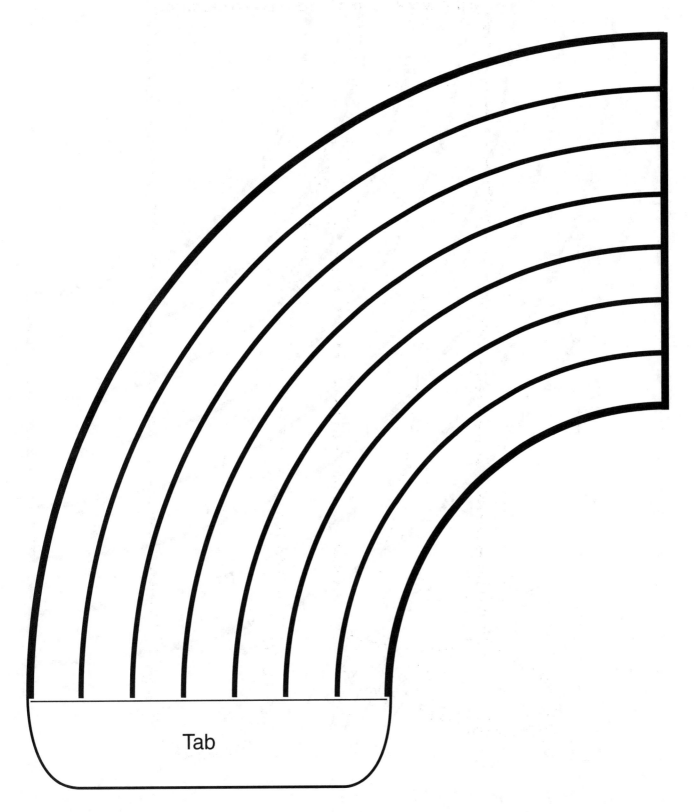

Tab

Rainbow *(cont.)*

108

Cupid

Use pages 111–112. Connect the Cupid at Tab A.
Add the wings at Tab B.

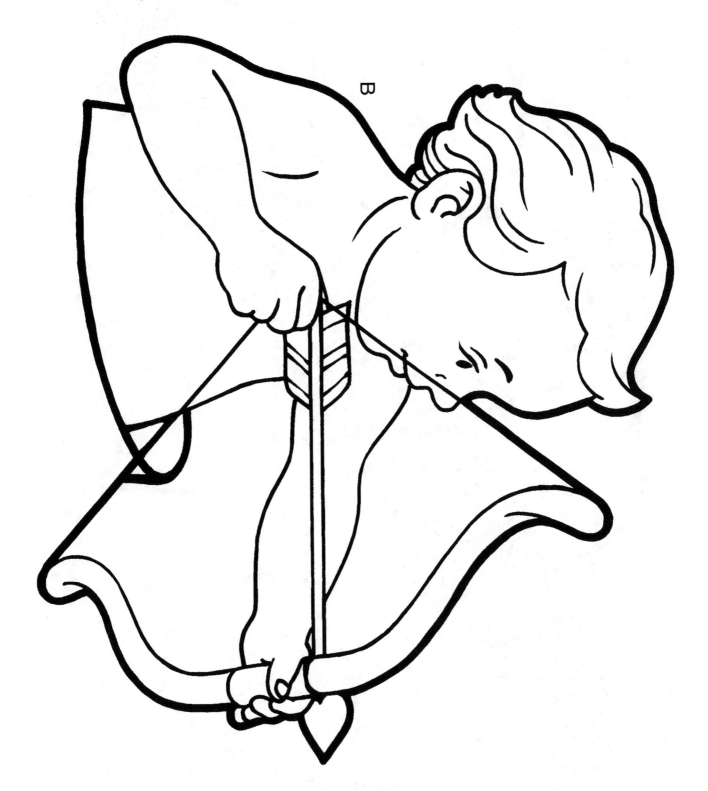

Cupid *(cont.)*

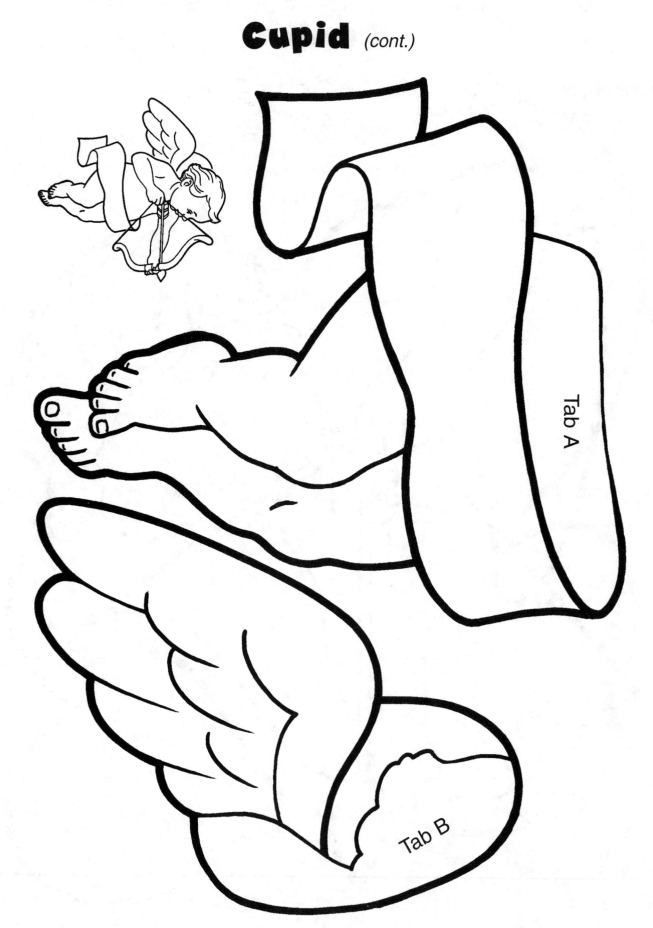

Tab A

Tab B

112

Hearts

Valentine Heart

Mailbox

Use pages 115–116. Connect the mailbox at the tab. Place flag in the desired position. Cut a strip of poster board if you want your mailbox to have a post.

Mailbox *(cont.)*

Tab

116

Envelope

Use pages 117–118. Fold down the three flaps. (See diagram.) Apply a small amount of glue to the flaps and press on the other envelope piece. When dry, place a valentine inside, and seal with a sticker.

Place glue here on flap.

Place glue here on flap.

Place glue here on flap.

Envelope *(cont.)*

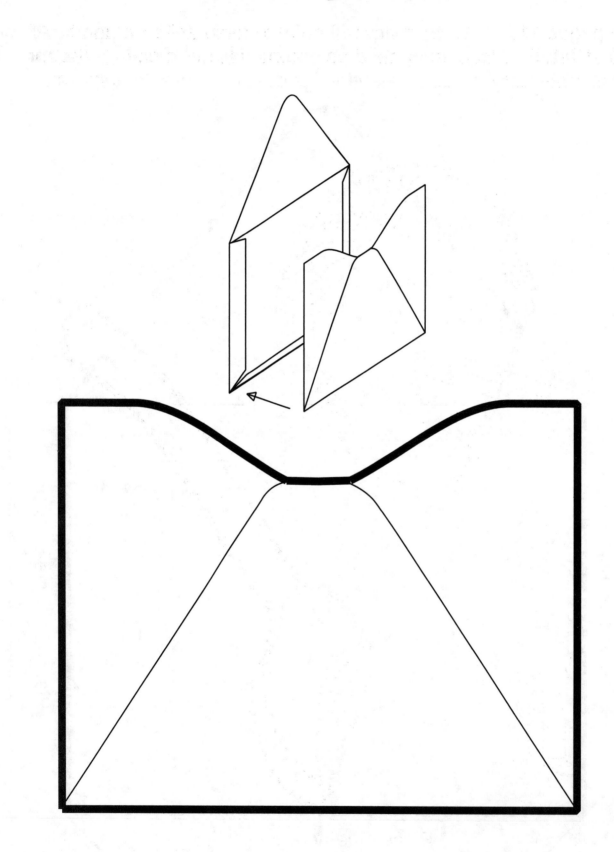

George Washington

Use pages 119–121. Connect the head to torso at Tab A and torso to legs at Tab B. Place ax in hand as shown. Use with cherry tree on pages 122–123.

George Washington *(cont.)*

Tab A

120

George Washington *(cont.)*

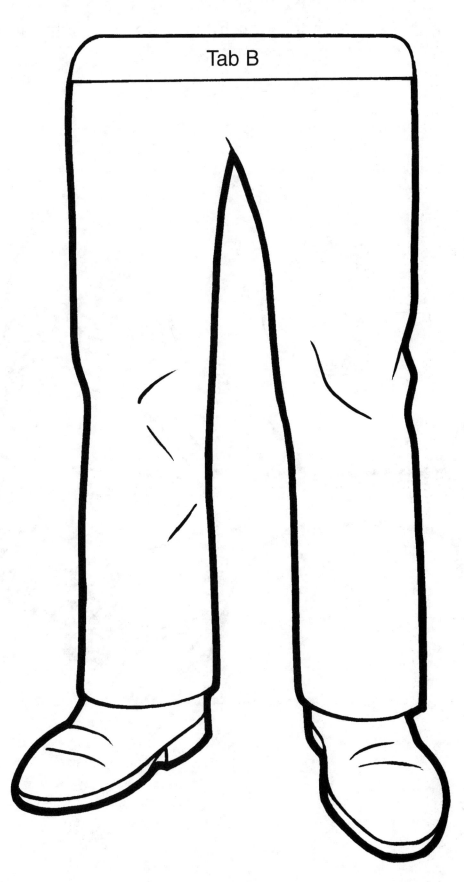

Tab B

Cherry Tree

Use pages 122–123. Overlap tree trunk at Tab A. Color and add cherries.

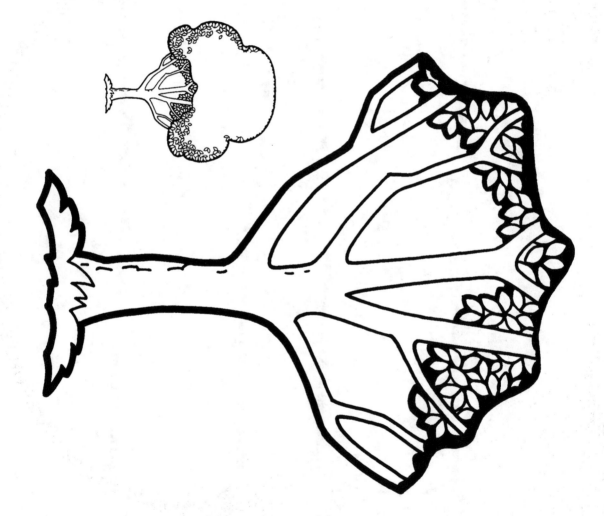

Log Cabin

Use pages 127–128. Connect the cabin at the tab.

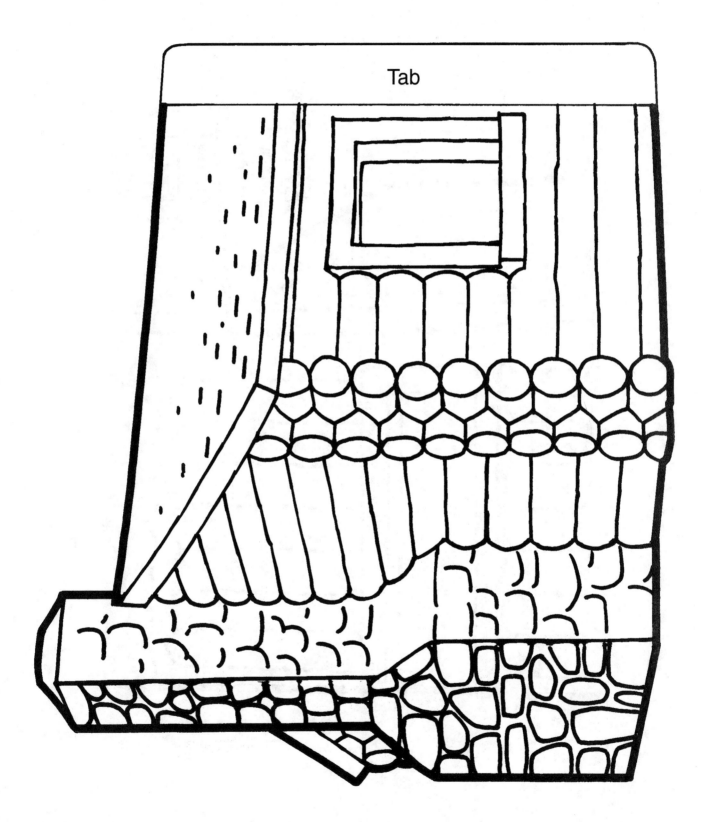

Log Cabin *(cont.)*

128

Leprechaun

Use pages 129–130. Overlap torso at the tab. Attach the walking stick to the left hand.

Leprechaun *(cont.)*

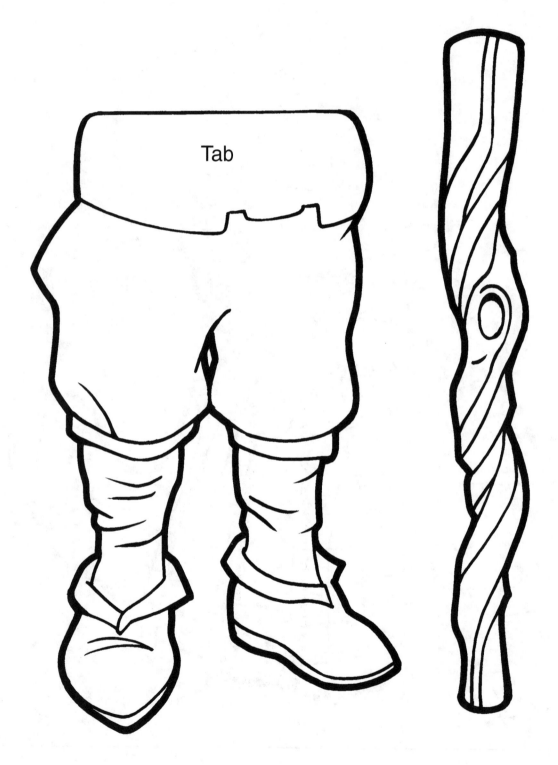

Tab

Robin

Use the robin with legs to stand near the nest on page 138, or cut nest on the dotted line and set the robin in the nest.

Nest and Eggs

Cut out eggs and arrange in nest. If they are robin's eggs, paint them blue! The robin is on page 137.

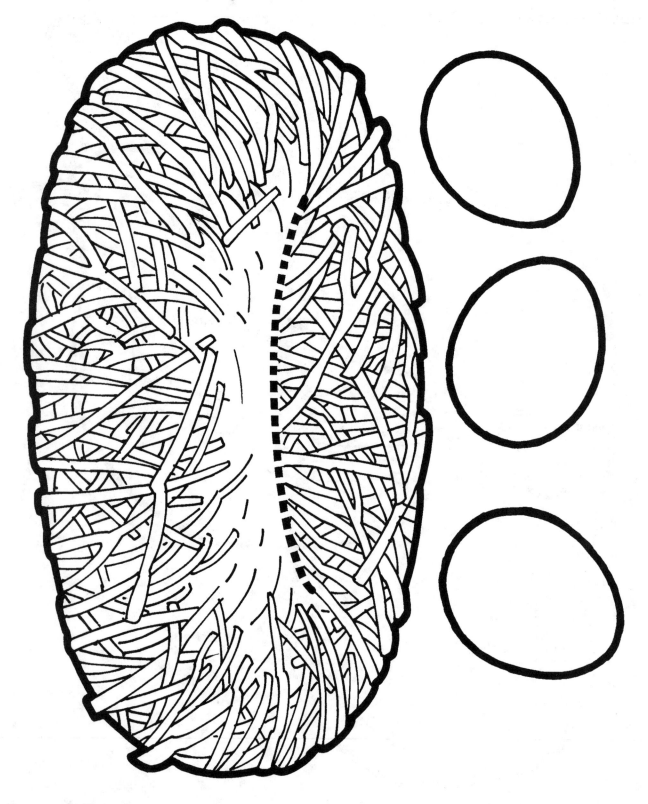

Spring Lamb

Use pages 139–140. Cut along the dotted lines to arrange the wreath around the lamb's neck. Attach the legs at tabs A, B, C, and D. Attach the tail with a brad.

Spring Lamb *(cont.)*

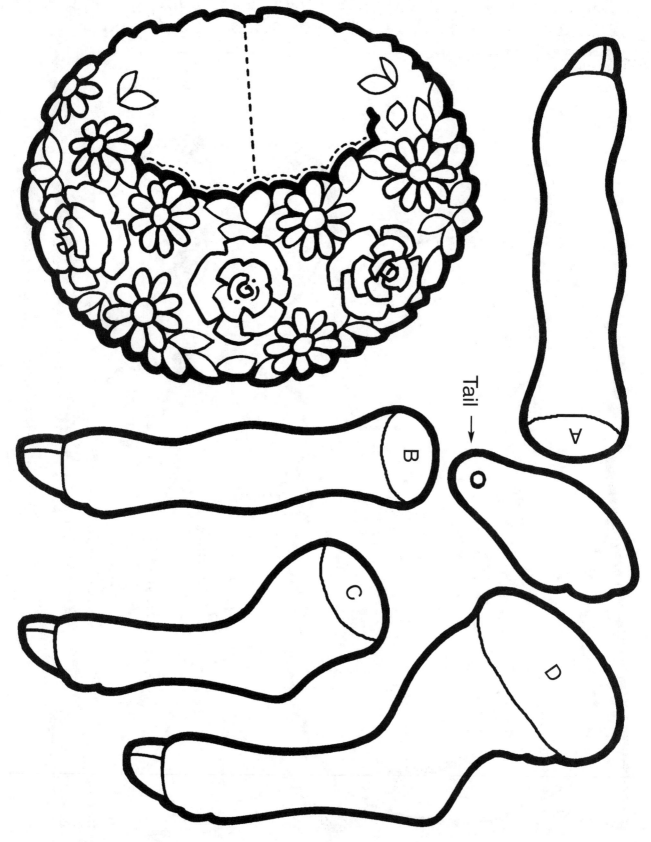

Daffodil

Color and cut out daffodil pieces. View diagram for placement of flower parts. If you are not planning to place the daffodil on a piece of background paper, use sturdy paper and overlap stem and leaves when gluing together.

Tulip

Color and cut out tulip pieces. View diagram for placement of flower parts. If you are not planning to place the tulip on a background piece of paper, use sturdy paper and overlap stem and leaves when gluing together.

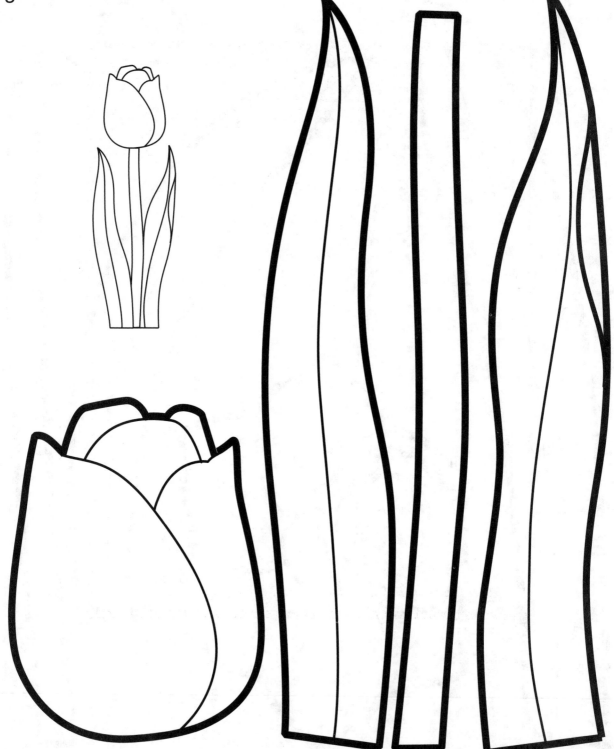

Seed Packet

Flower Pot

Use with flowers on pages 141–142.

144

Beehive

Use pages 145–146

Bees

Inchworm

Use pages 147–148. Connect the large inchworm at the tab. The fully assembled inchworm will be one foot long. Combine the six small inchworms from each page on a twelve-inch strip of paper and make a ruler.

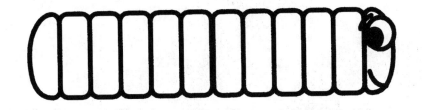

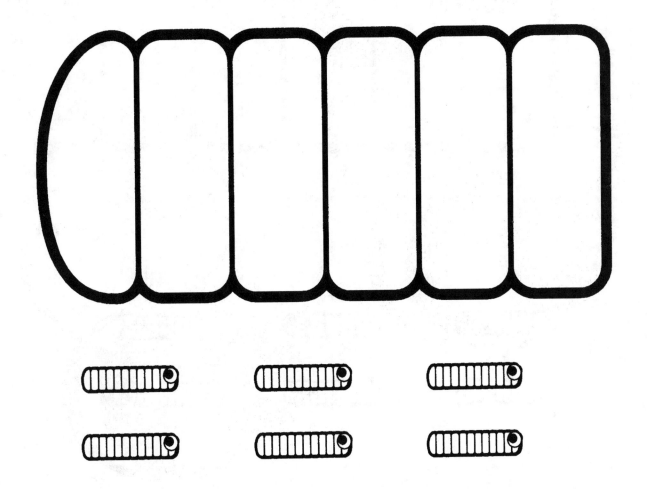

Inchworm *(cont.)*

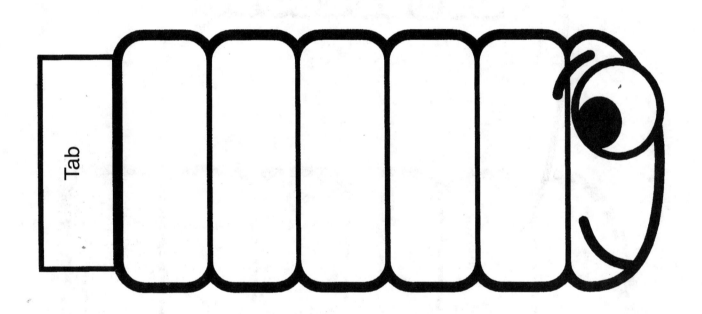

Tab

Butterfly

Use pages 149–151. Color and then cut out the pieces. Place a small amount of glue over the A on the body section. Attach the wings to the butterfly body by aligning the wings over A. Once attached, bend legs down.

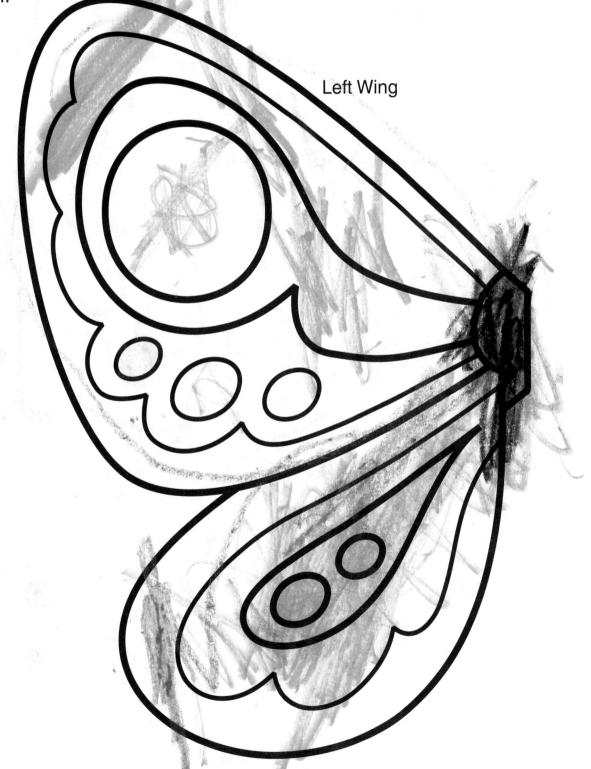

Left Wing

Butterfly *(cont.)*

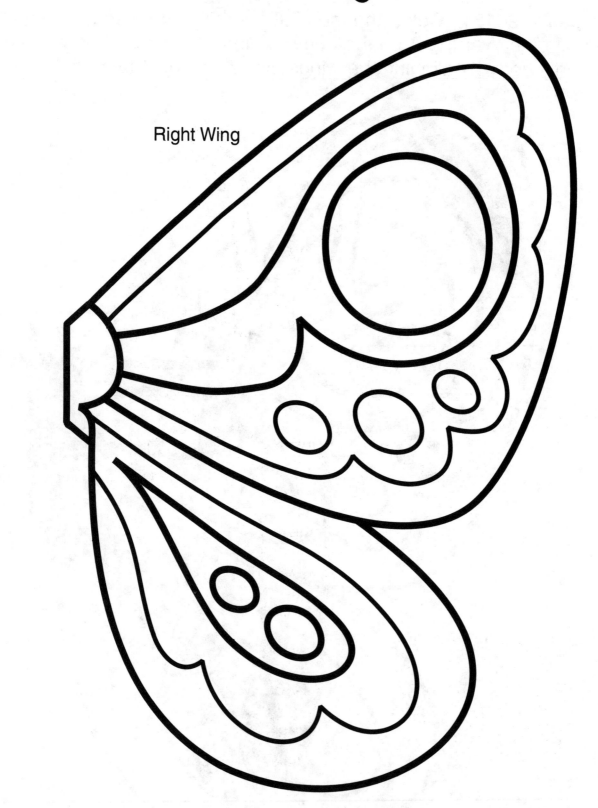

Right Wing

150

Butterfly *(cont.)*

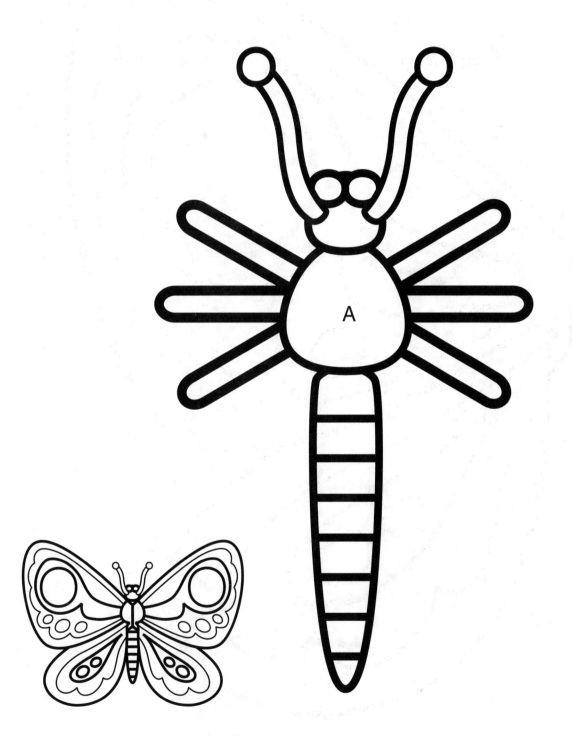

Hen and Chick

152

Pig and Piglet

Cow

Duck and Duckling

Horse

Barn

Use pages 157 and 158. Connect the barn at the tab. Cut barn doors on solid lines and fold back at dotted lines to open. Use the animals from pages 152–156 and the silo and the haystack on pages 163–164 to complete the farm scene.

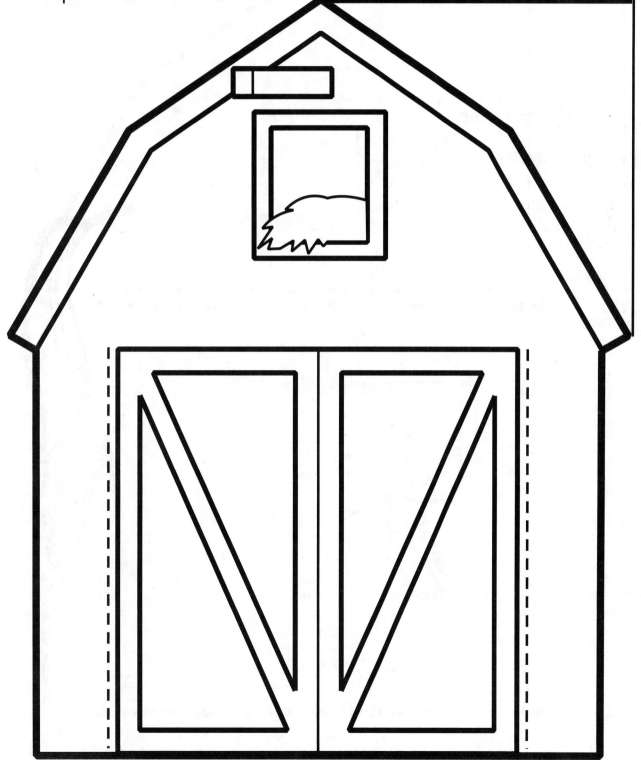

Barn *(cont.)*

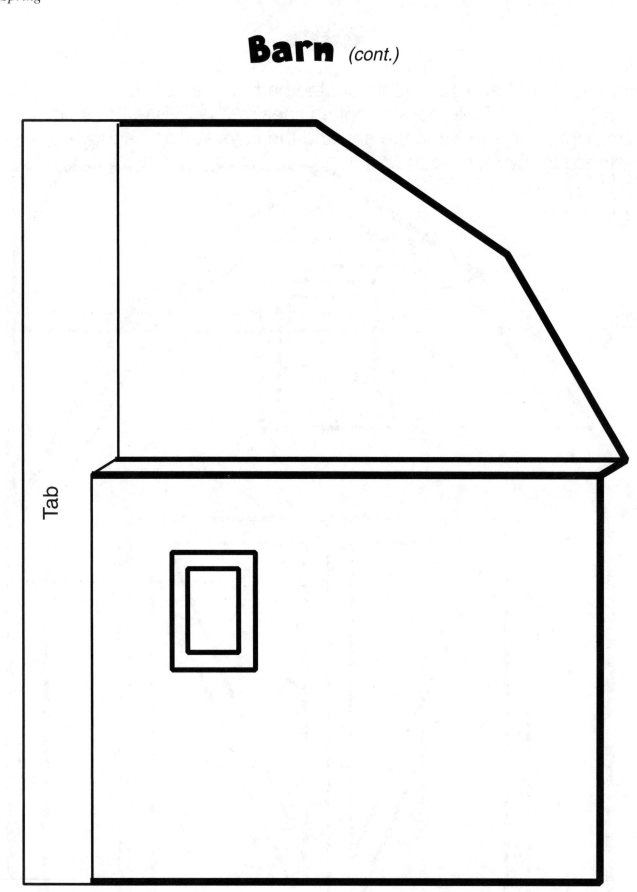

Tab

Silo

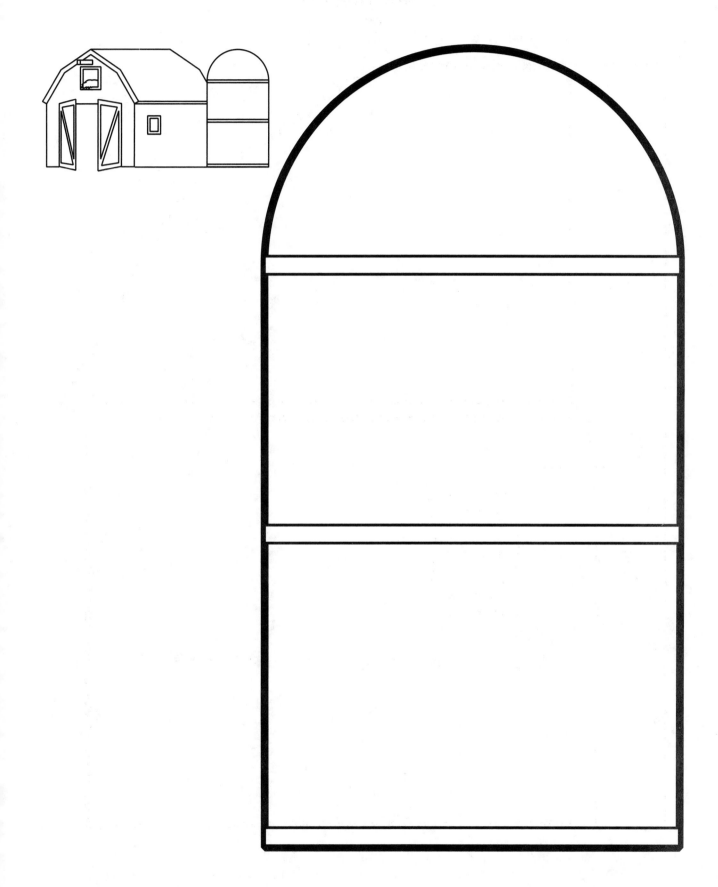

Hay Stack

Use with the barn on pages 157–159.

Kite

Use pages 161–162. Connect the kite at the tab.

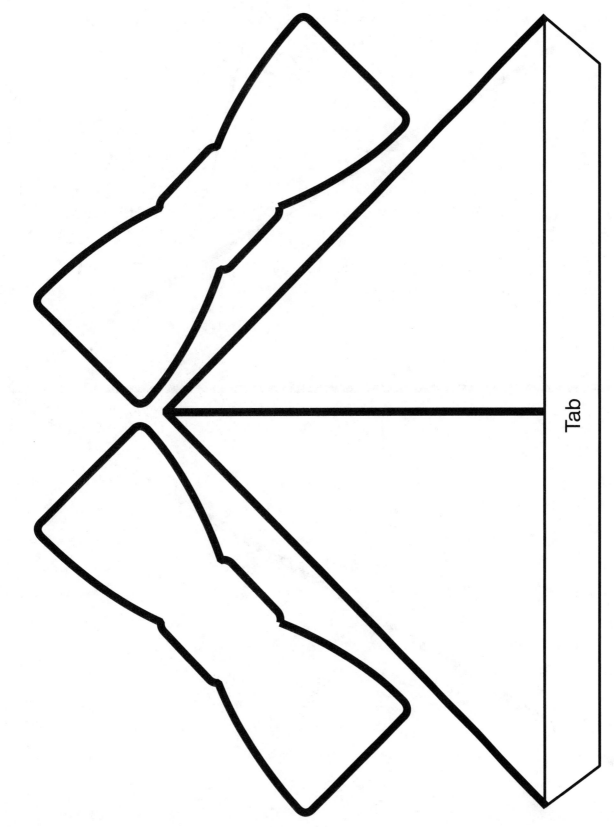

Tab

Kite *(cont.)*

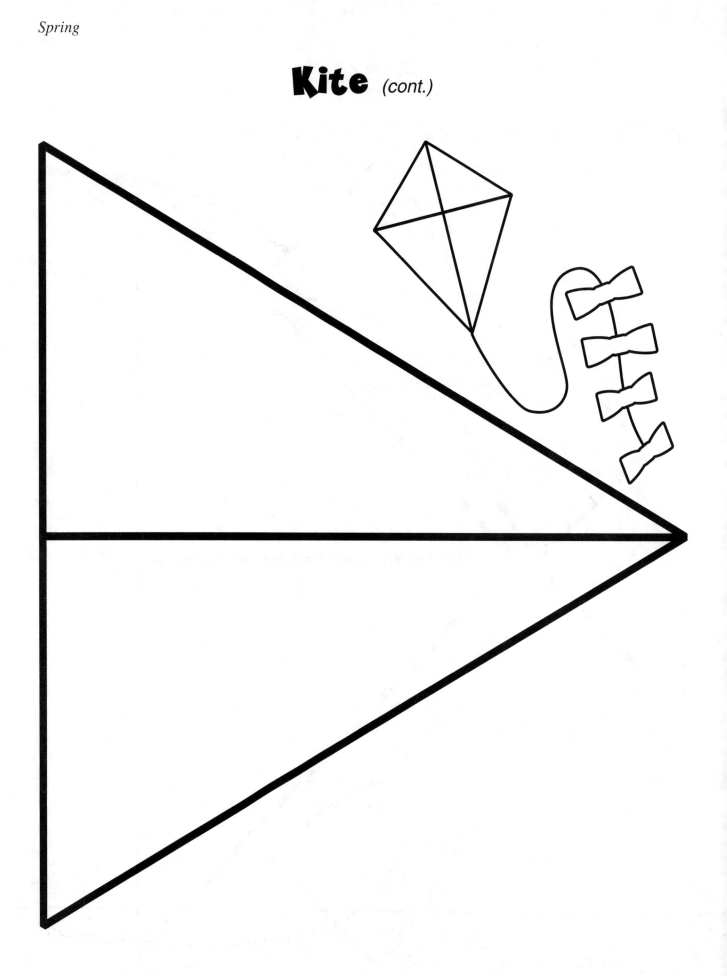

Cloud

Use pages 163–164.   Connect the cloud at the tab.

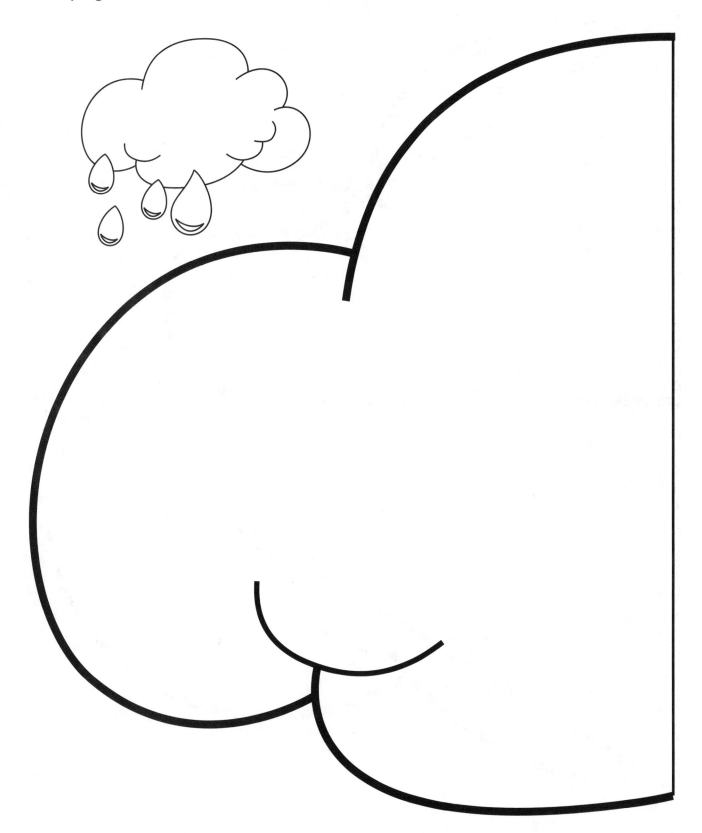

Cloud *(cont.)*

Tab

Raindrops

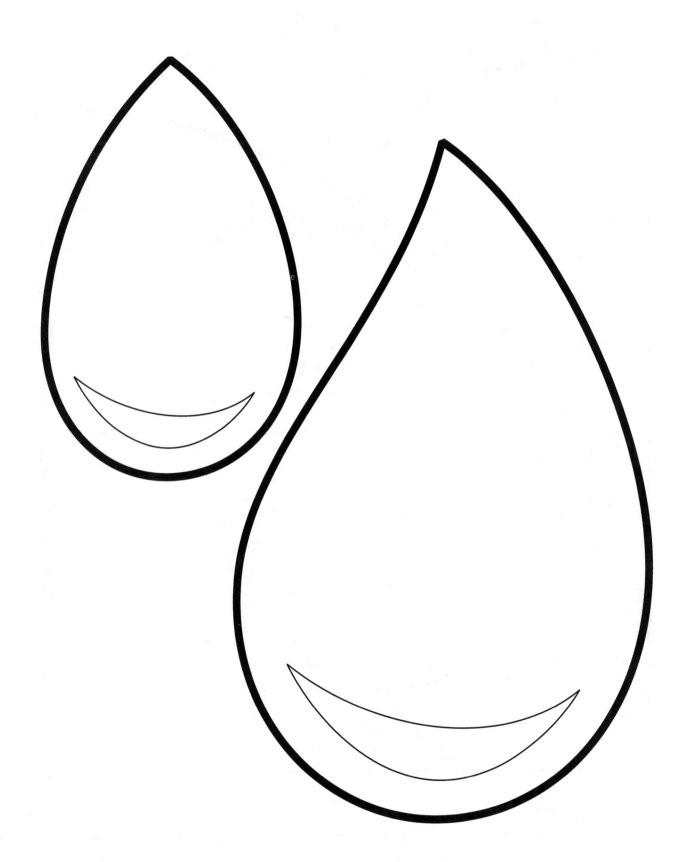

Umbrella

Use pages 166–168. Connect the umbrella at Tab A. Connect the handle at Tab B and attach it to the umbrella.

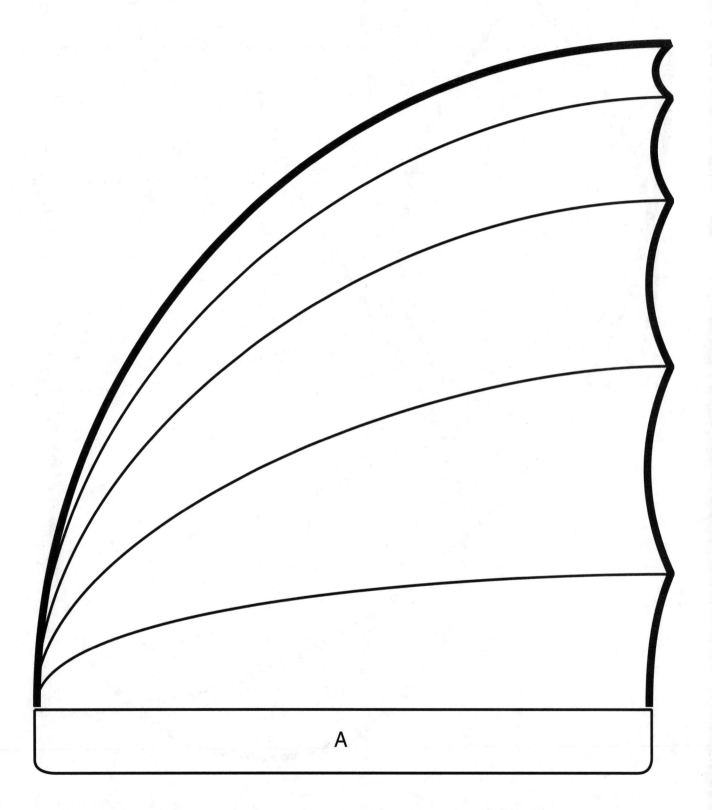

A

Umbrella *(cont.)*

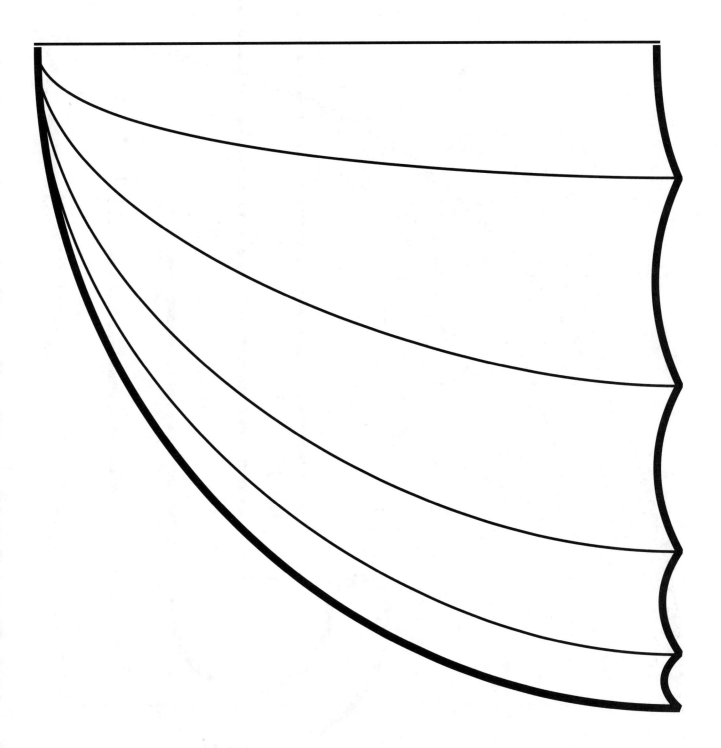

Umbrella *(cont.)*

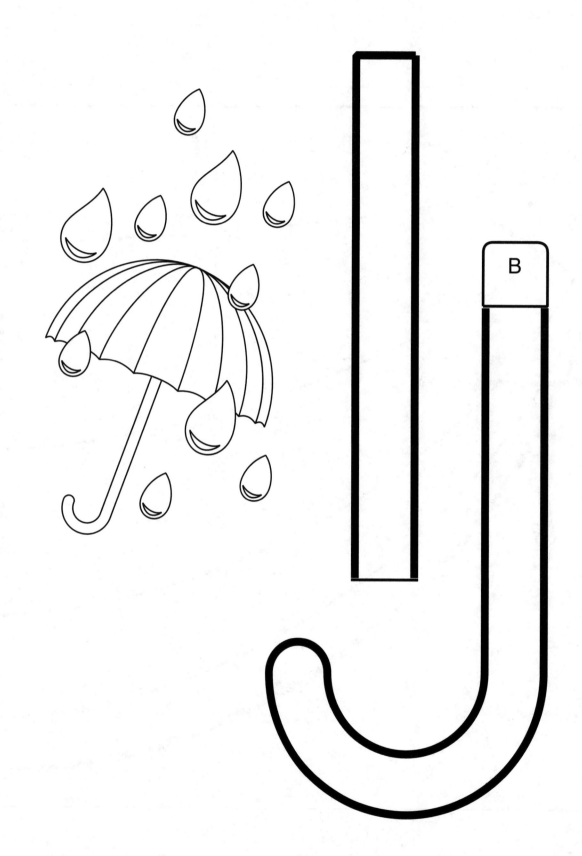

Small Bunnies

Easter Bunny

Use pages 170–172. Overlap the neck and attach it to Tab A. (You may wish to cut off the black line at the end of the neck.) Attach the tail at Tab B. Place the apron and then add the arms at C & D. Be careful to place the paintbrush before completely gluing down the arm.

Easter Bunny *(cont.)*

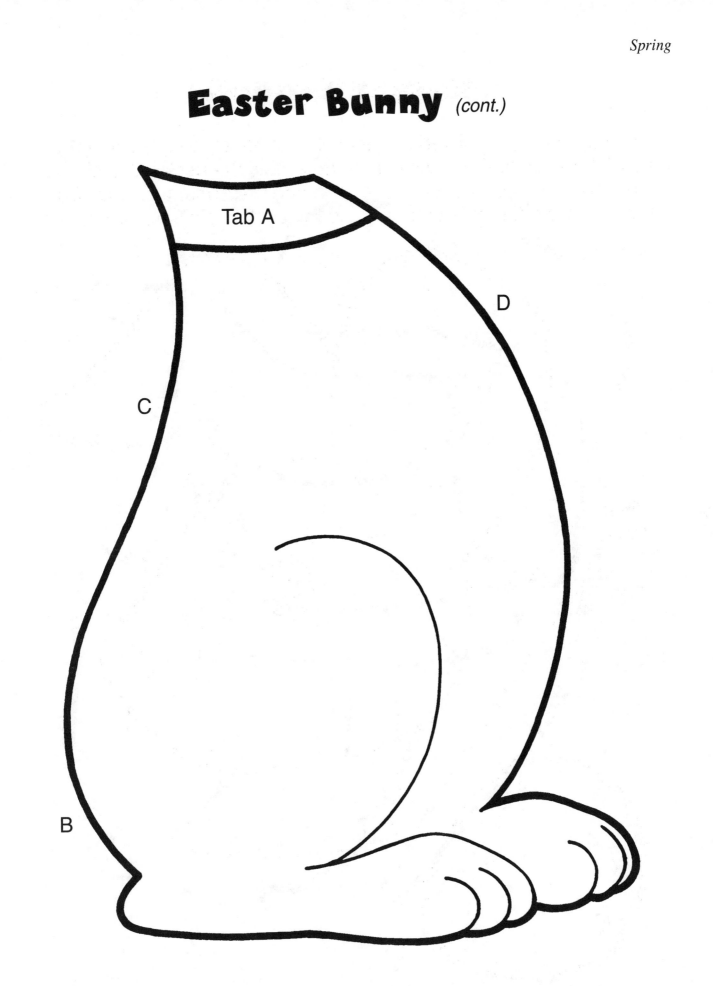

Easter Bunny *(cont.)*

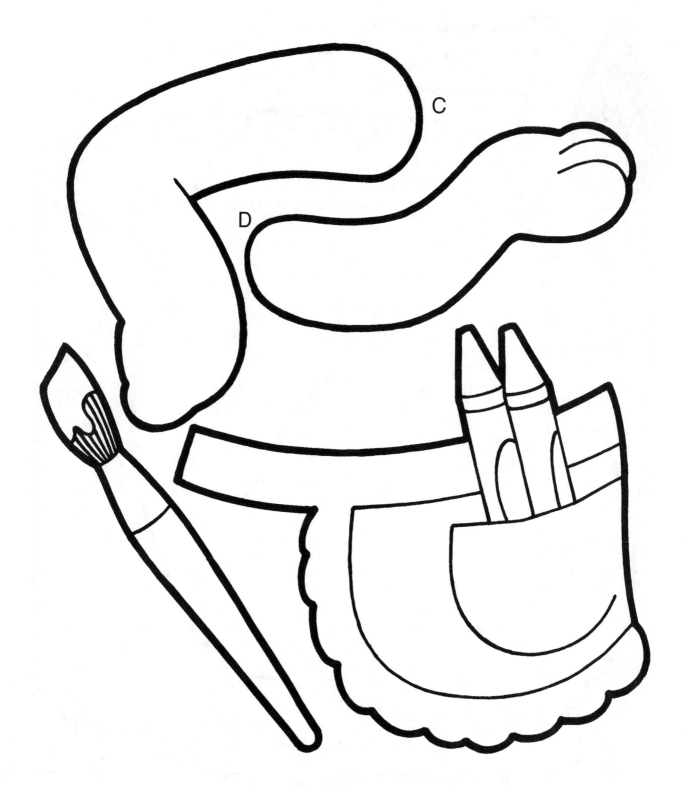

Paint Can and Brush

Plain Egg and Carrot

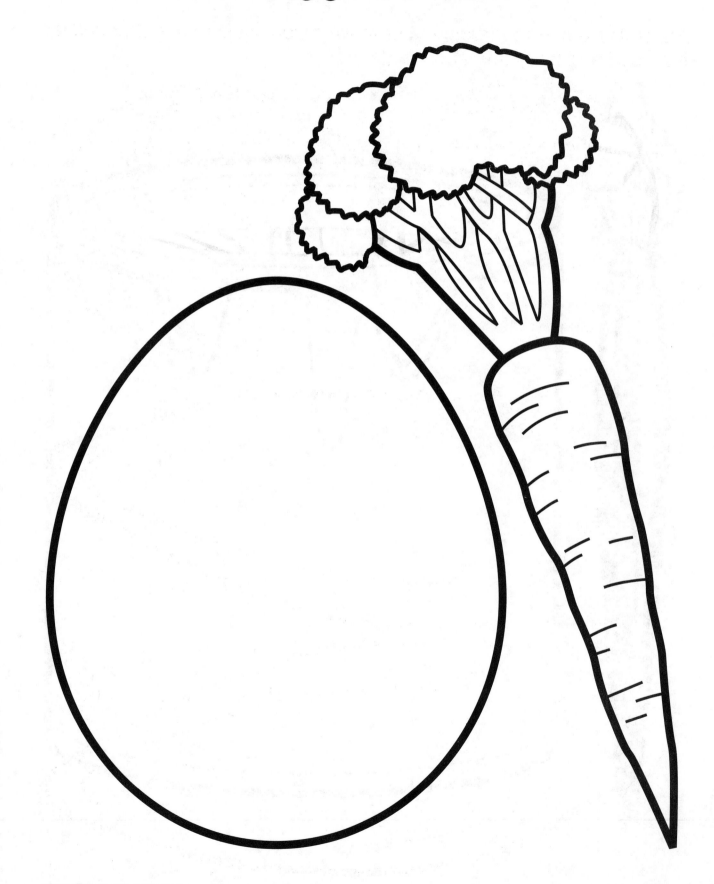

Bunny Ears and Eggs

Attach the ears to a headband or make a bunny using paper plates for the head and body and add the ears.

Easter Egg

Basket

Use pages 177–178. Connect the handle to the basket at A and B. Attach the bow if desired and fill with colored eggs (page 175) or flowers (pages 141, 142, 180 and 186).

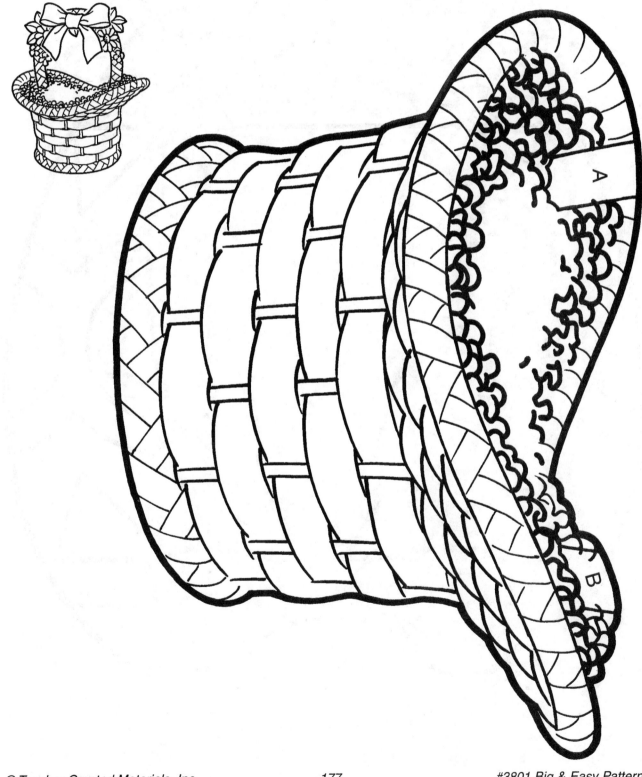

Basket (cont.)

A

B

178

I Love You, Mom

Rose

Color and cut out the rose pieces. View diagram for placement of flower parts. If you are not planning to place the rose on a piece of background paper, use sturdy paper and overlap stem and leaves when gluing together.

Bow

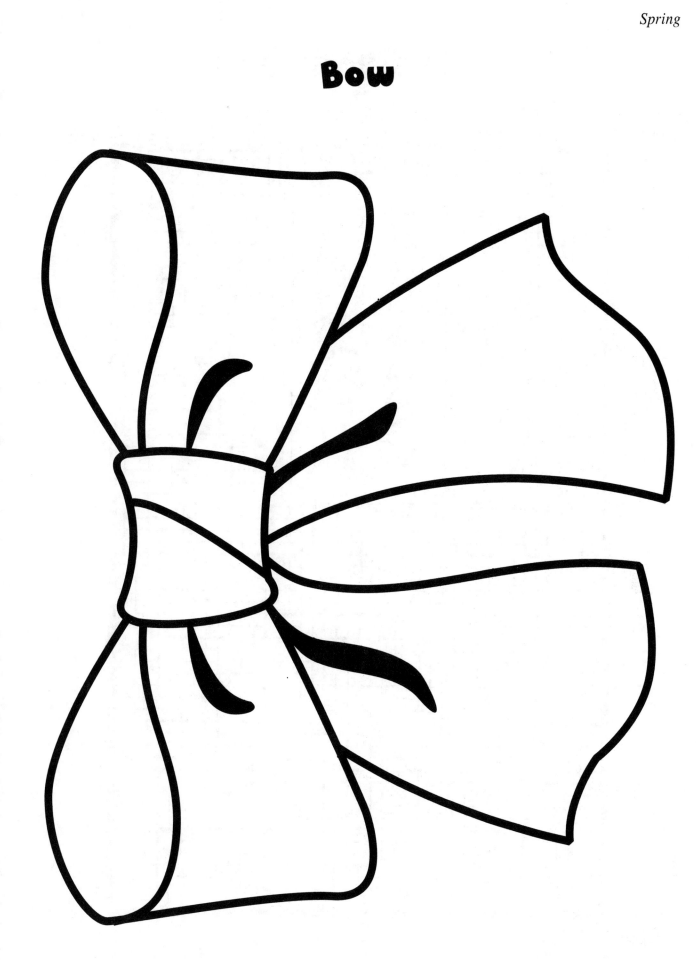

I Love You, Dad

Tie

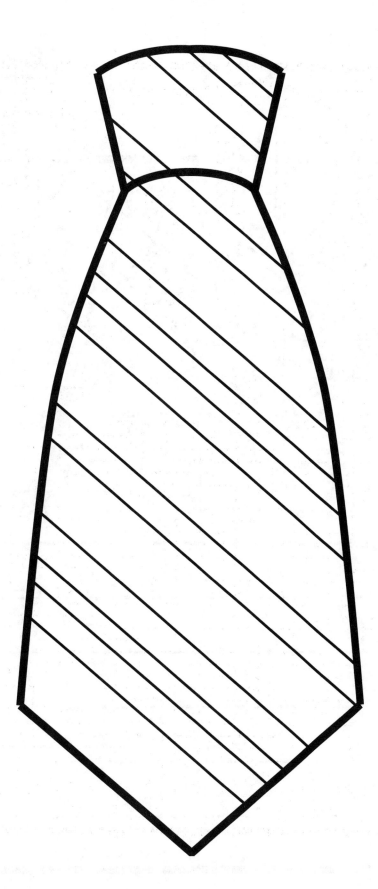

American Flag

Use pages 184–185.

Connect the flag at the tab.

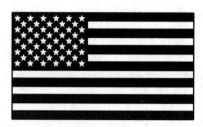

American Flag *(cont.)*

Tab

Poppy

Color and cut out the poppy pieces. View diagram for placement of flower parts. If you are not planning to place the poppy on a piece of background paper, copy onto sturdy paper and overlap stem and leaves when gluing together.

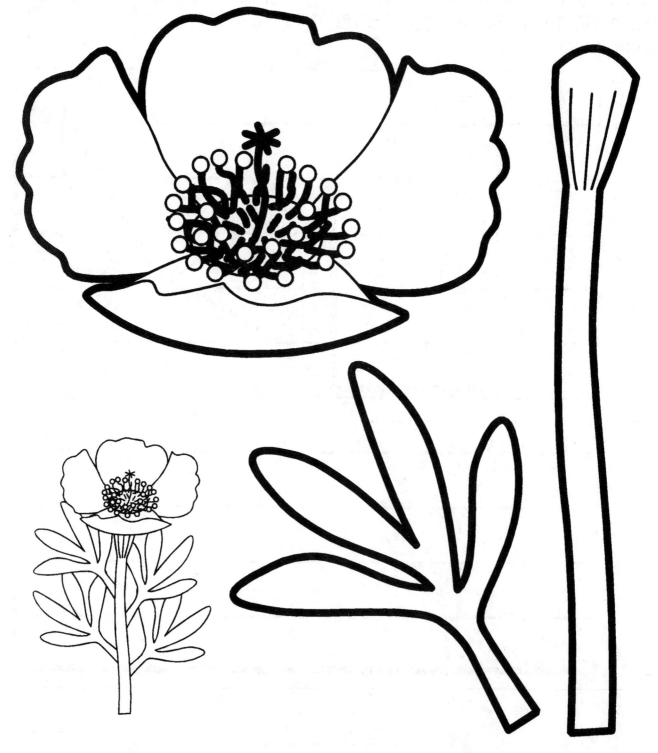

186

Sun

Use pages 187–190. The four-page sun pattern is put together in a circular fashion.

Attach Tab A. It becomes the upper left quadrant. The sun section marked by Tab B becomes the lower left quadrant. Next, attach the sun section marked with Tab C at the lower right quadrant. Finally, place the quadrant marked with Tab D in the remaining space to complete the sun.

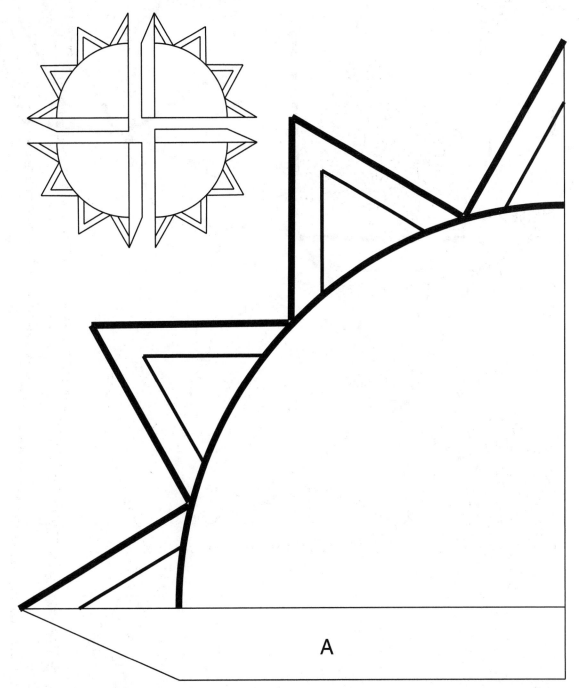

A

Sun *(cont.)*

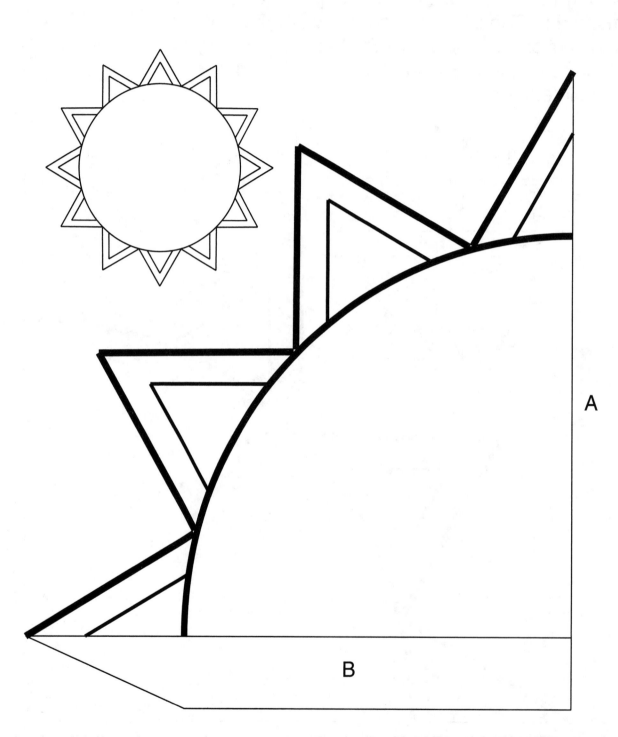

A

B

Sun *(cont.)*

C

Sun *(cont.)*

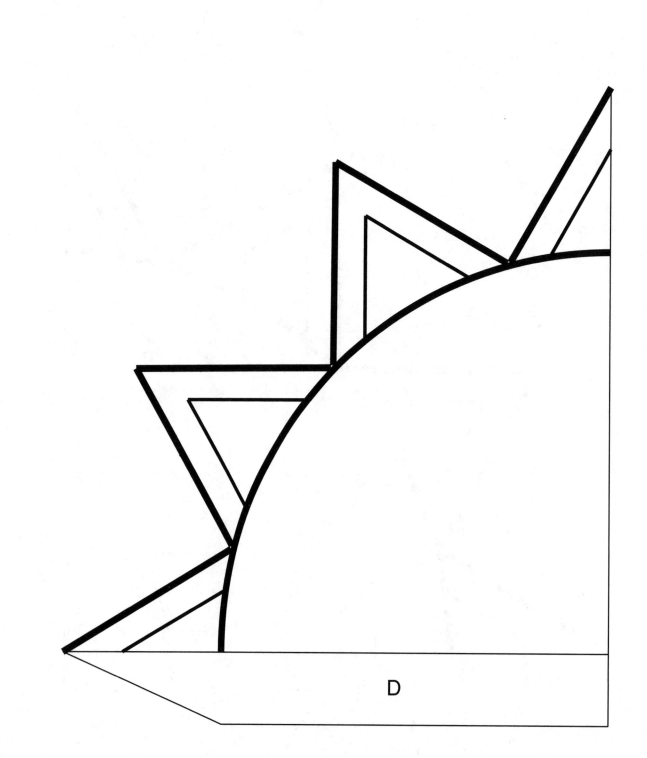

D

Sea Horse

Sea Shells

Starfish

Fish

Tropical Fish

Seagull

Use pages 196–198. Attach the right wing at Tab A and the left wing at Tab B.

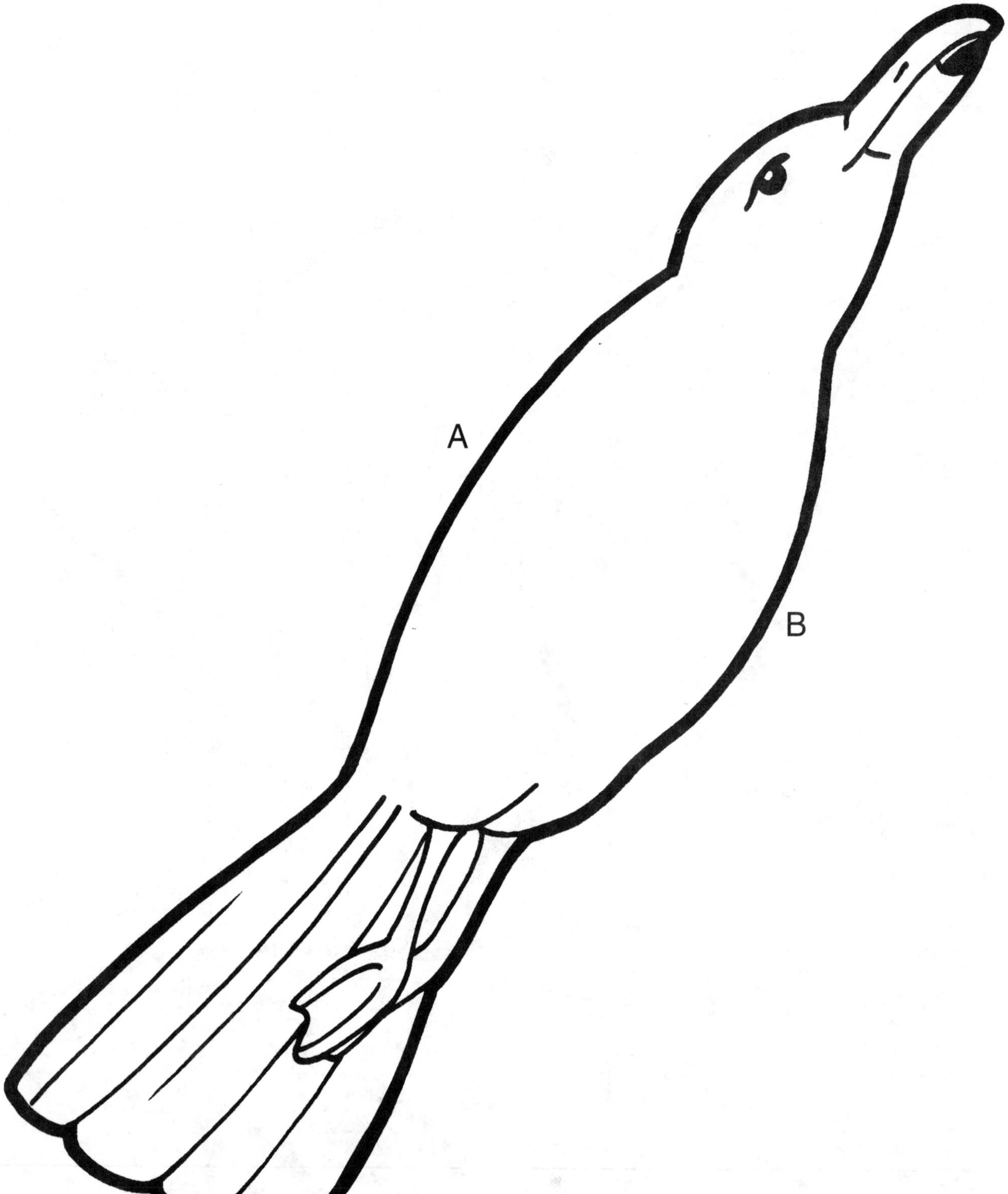

A

B

196

Seagull *(cont.)*

Tab B

Seagull *(cont.)*

Tab A

198

Crab

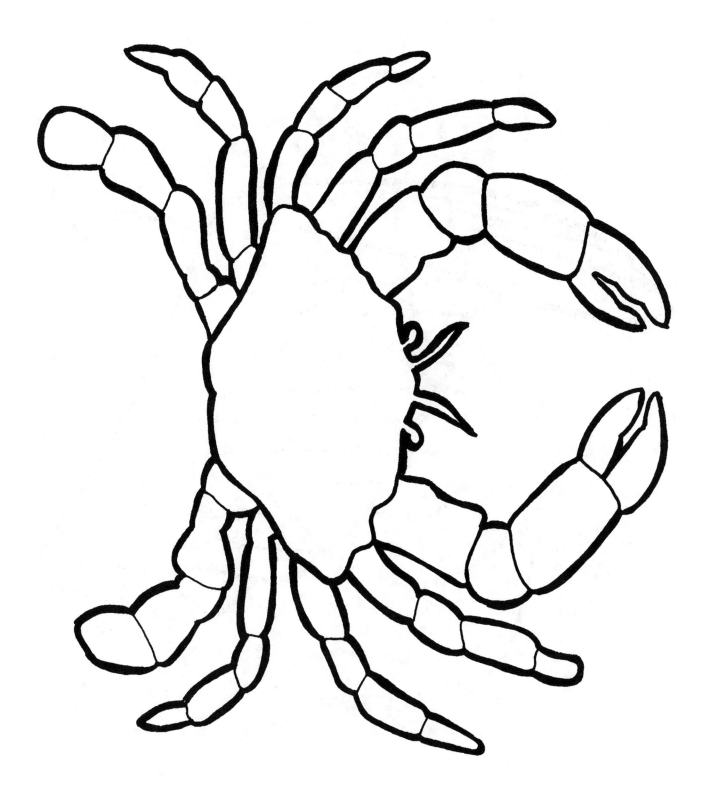

Octopus

Use pages 200–201. Connect the octopus at the tab.

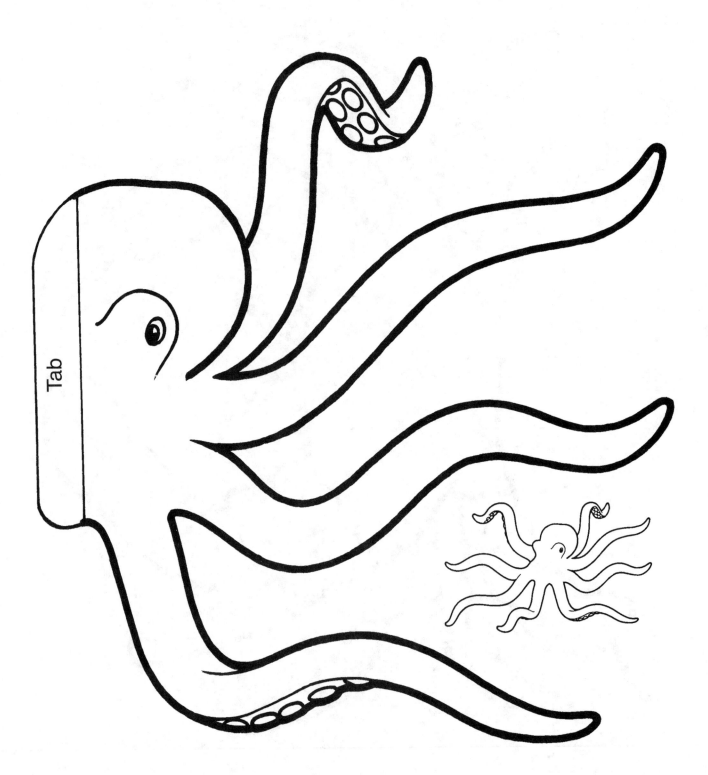

Octopus *(cont.)*

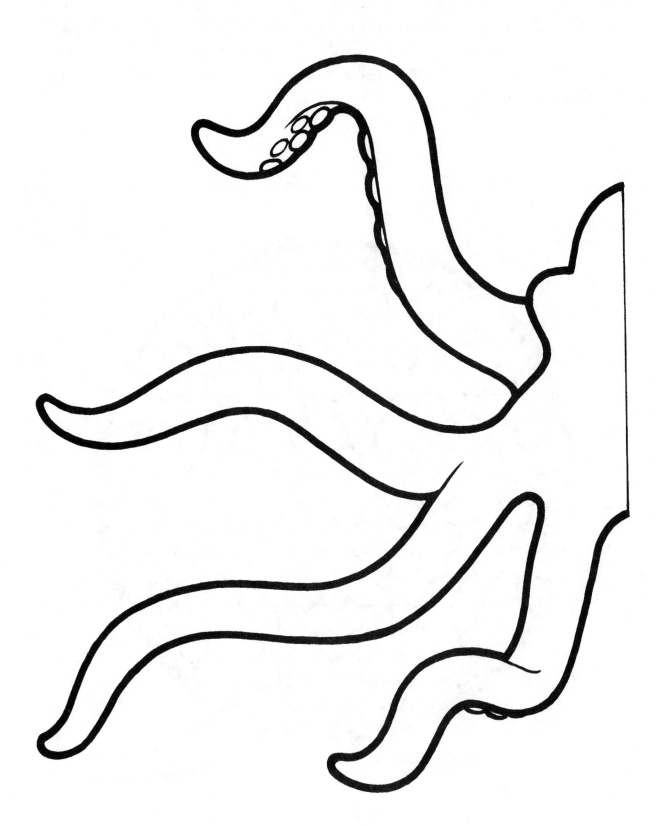

Sunflower

Use pages 202–203. Copy seed head on brown paper and cover with sunflower seeds. You will need approximately 25 petals to complete the flower. Use yellow paper and the petal pattern on page 203 to create your petals. Paint a small stick green or use green paper for the stem and leaves.

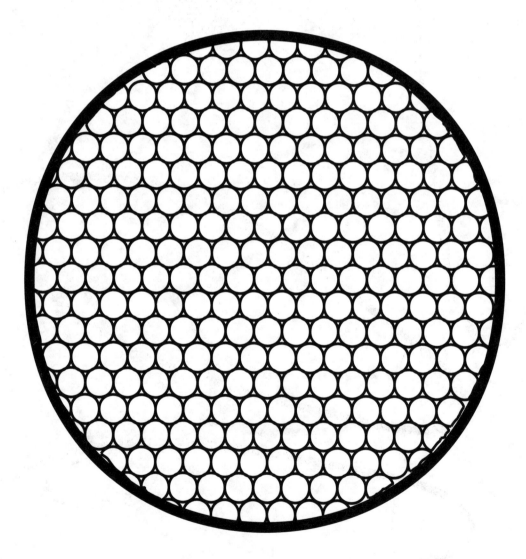

Sunflower *(cont.)*

Swim Trunks

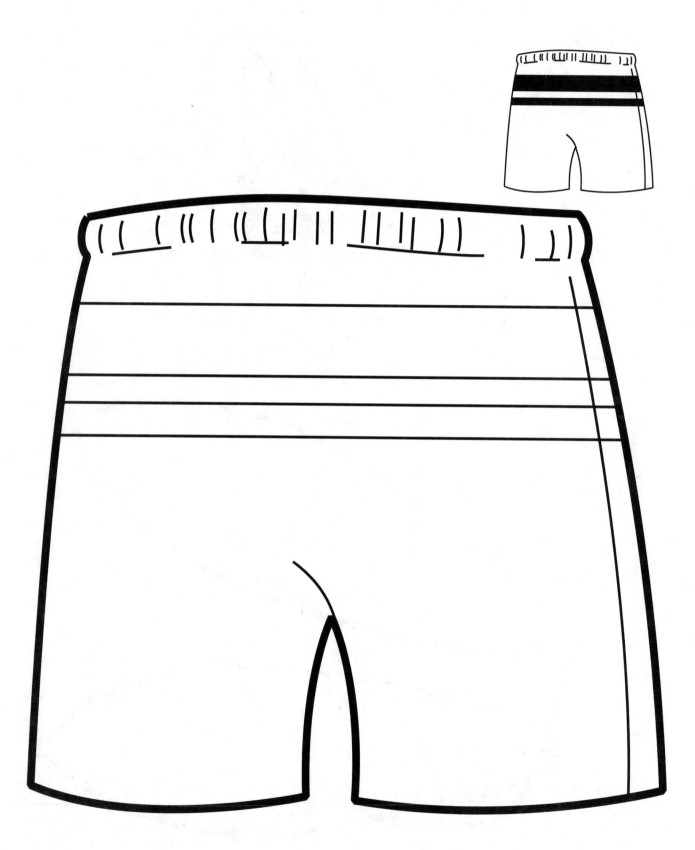

Swimsuit

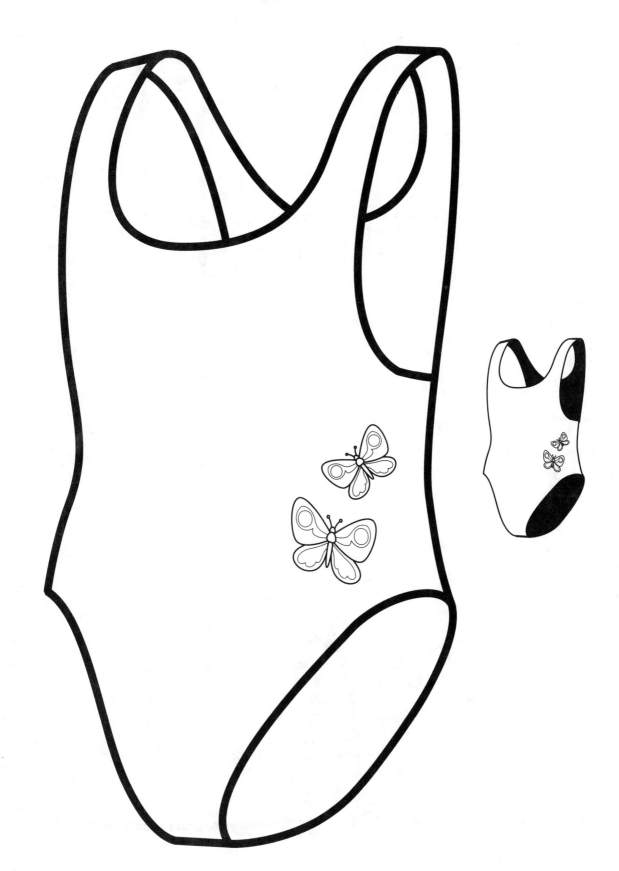

205 #3801 Big & Easy Patterns

Snorkel

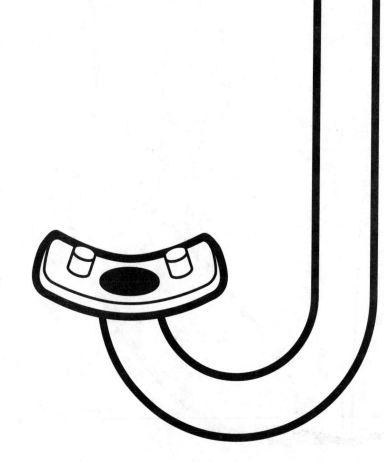

Fins

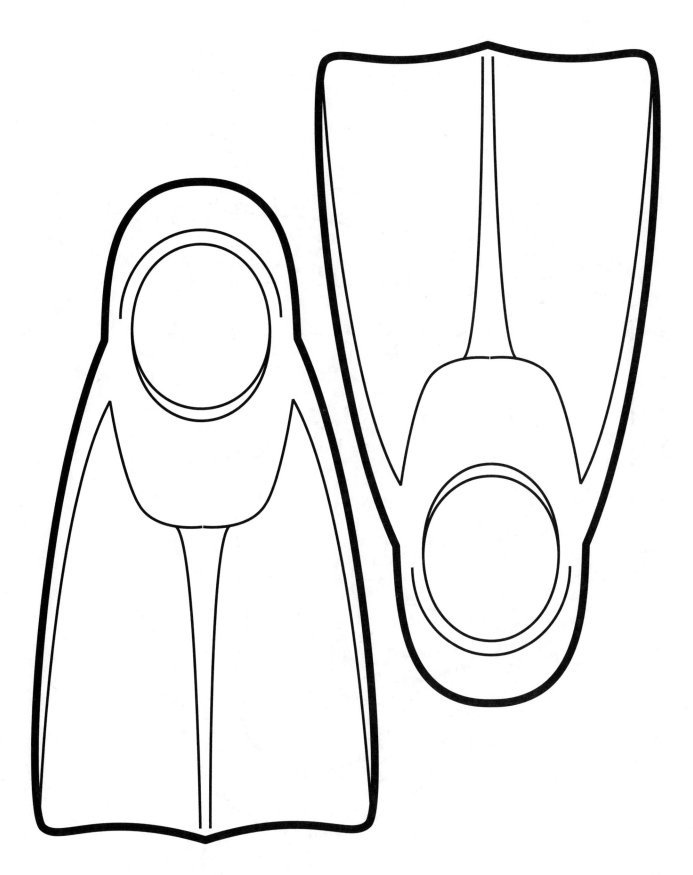

Mask

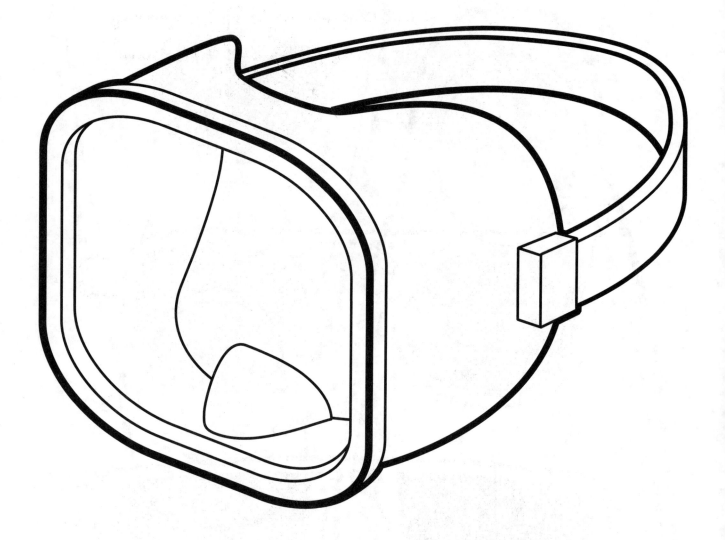

Sunglasses

Use pages 209–210. Bend tabs at the end of the lenses and attach sides. (See diagram on page 210.)

Sunglasses (cont.)

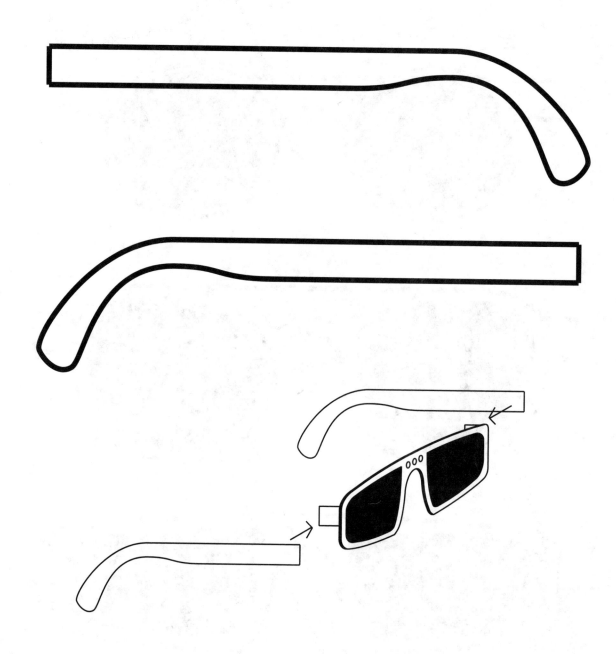

210

Sand Shovel

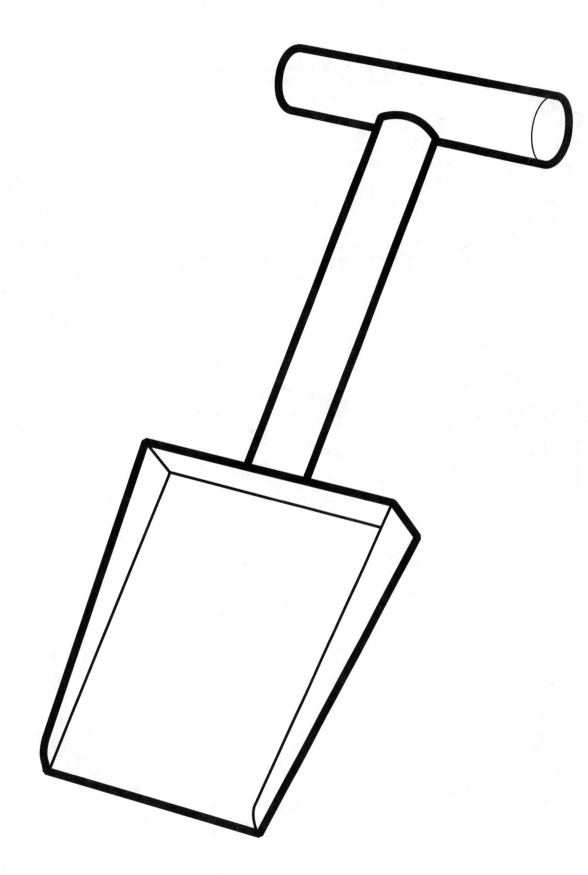

Sand Pail

212

Ice Cream Scooper

Fireworks

Use pages 216–217. Connect to the tab. Decorate with glitter.

Fireworks *(cont.)*

Tab A

Hot Dog

Cut a slit in the bun on the dotted line to slip in the hot dog. Glue on red and yellow yarn for ketchup and mustard.

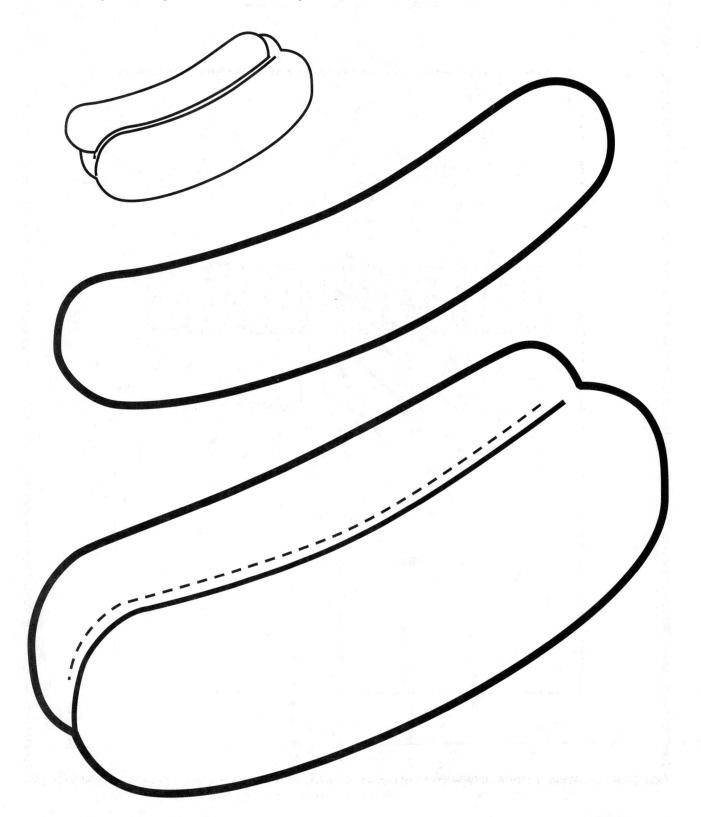

Autograph Album

Fountain Pen

Attach pen cap to the tab.

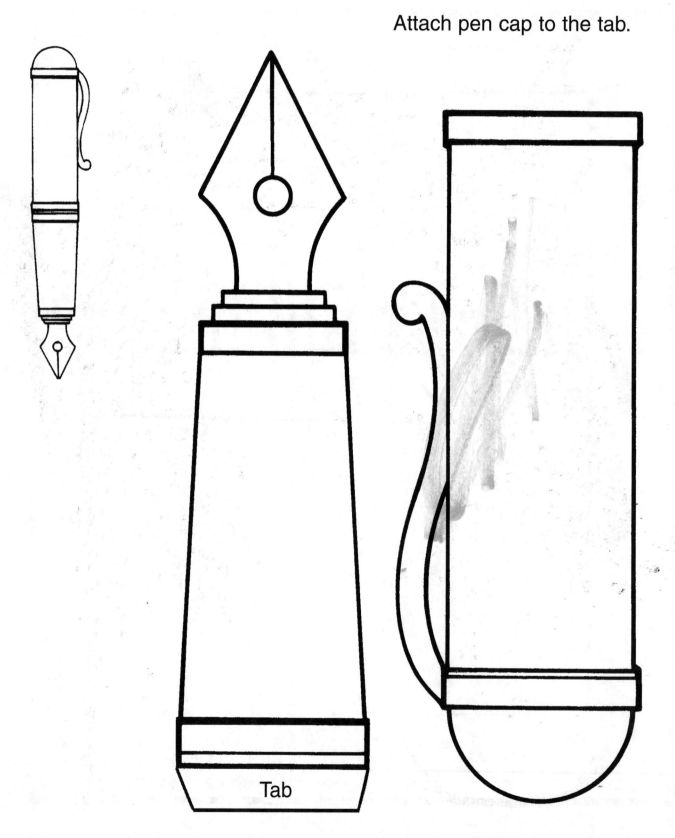

Tab

Little Miss Muffet

Use pages 249–251. Connect Miss Muffet at the tab. Cut out the spider and bowl and arrange as desired.

Tab

Little Miss Muffet (cont.)

250

Little Miss Muffet (cont.)

Humpty Dumpty

Use pages 252–254.

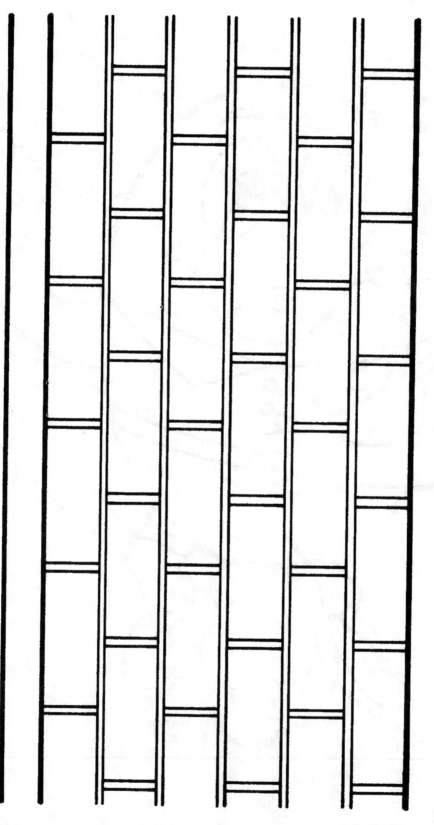

Humpty Dumpty (cont.)

Humpty Dumpty *(cont.)*

The Three Little Kittens

Use pages 255–257.

The Three Little Kittens *(cont.)*

Mother

Baa, Baa, Black Sheep

Use pages 259–261. Connect the sheep at the tab and color black.
Use with the bag of wool on page 261.

Tab

Baa, Baa, Black Sheep *(cont.)*

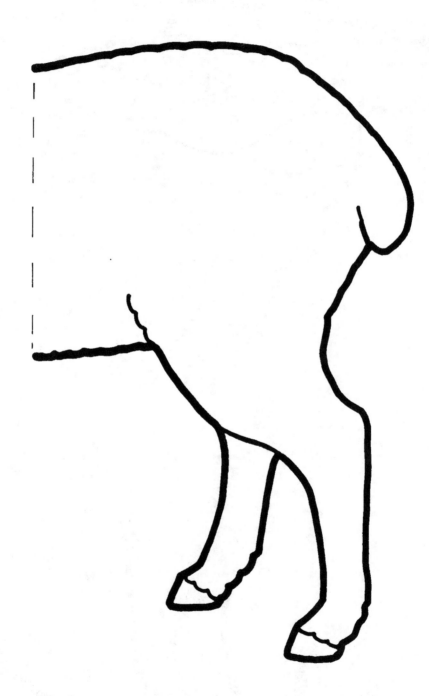

Baa, Baa, Black Sheep *(cont.)*

Make three bags and color the wool black. The bags may be any color.

Hickory Dickory Dock

Use pages 262–264. Connect the clock at the tab. Attach the hands and the mouse from page 264.

Hickory Dickory Dock (cont.)

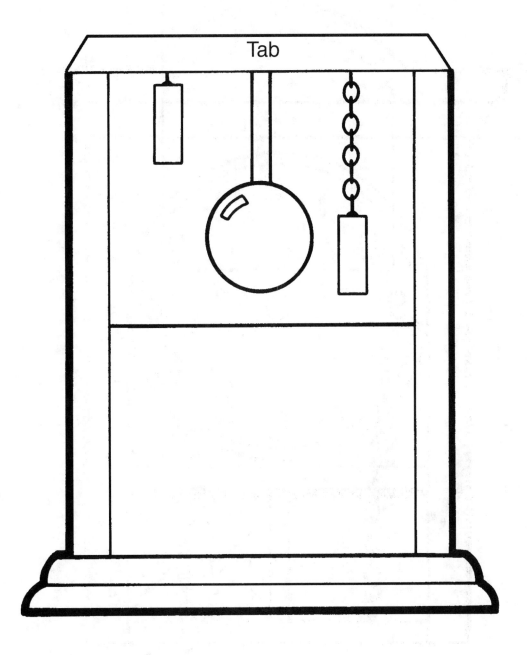

Tab

Hickory Dickory Dock *(cont.)*

Use a brad to attach the hands to the clock.

White House

Use pages 265–266. Cut out and connect at the tab.

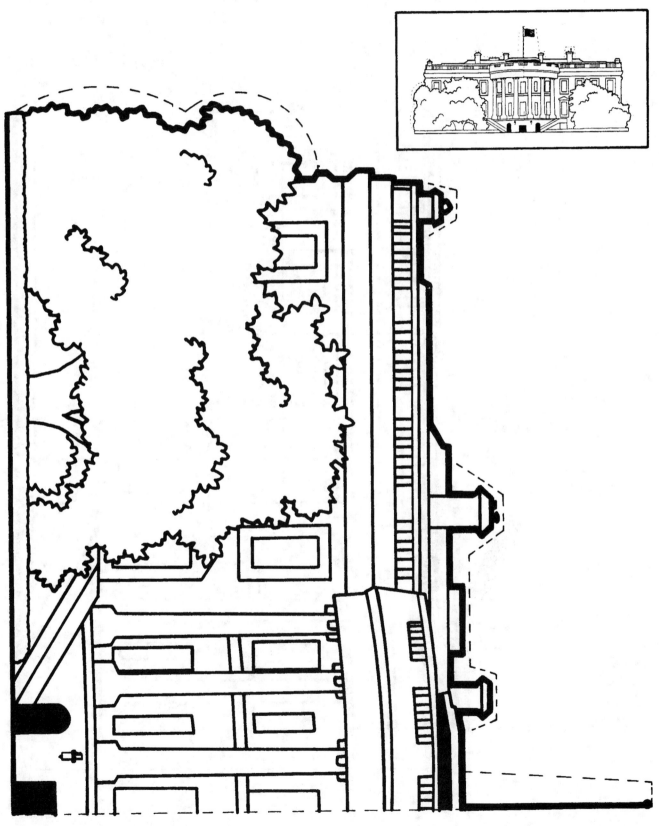

White House (cont.)

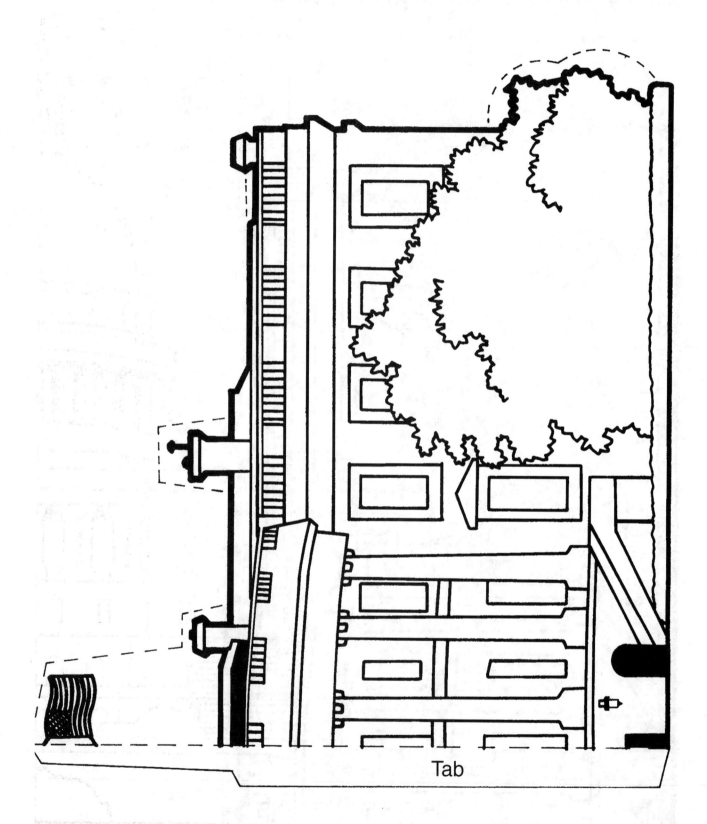

Tab

Capitol

Use pages 267–268. Cut out and connect at the tab.

Capitol *(cont.)*

Tab

Eagle

Use pages 269–270. Attach wings behind the eagle at the tabs.

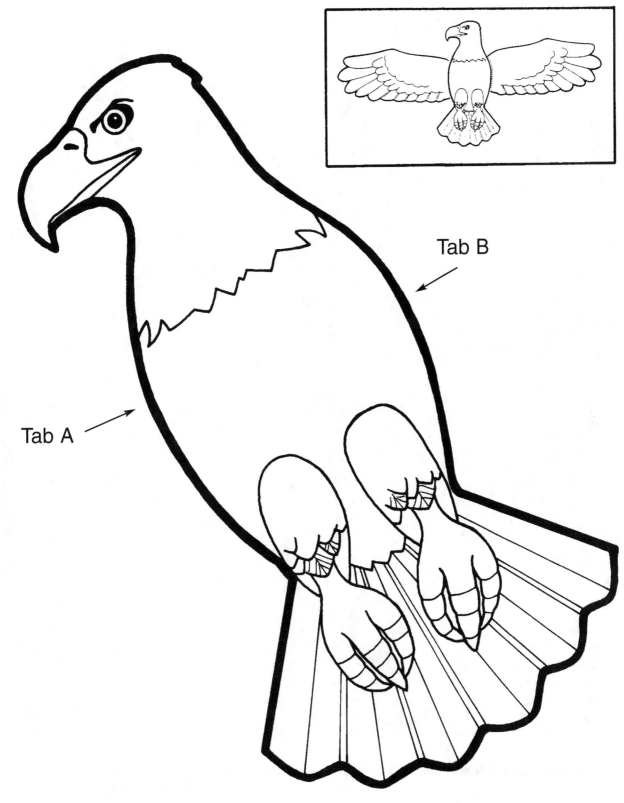

Tab B

Tab A

Eagle *(cont.)*

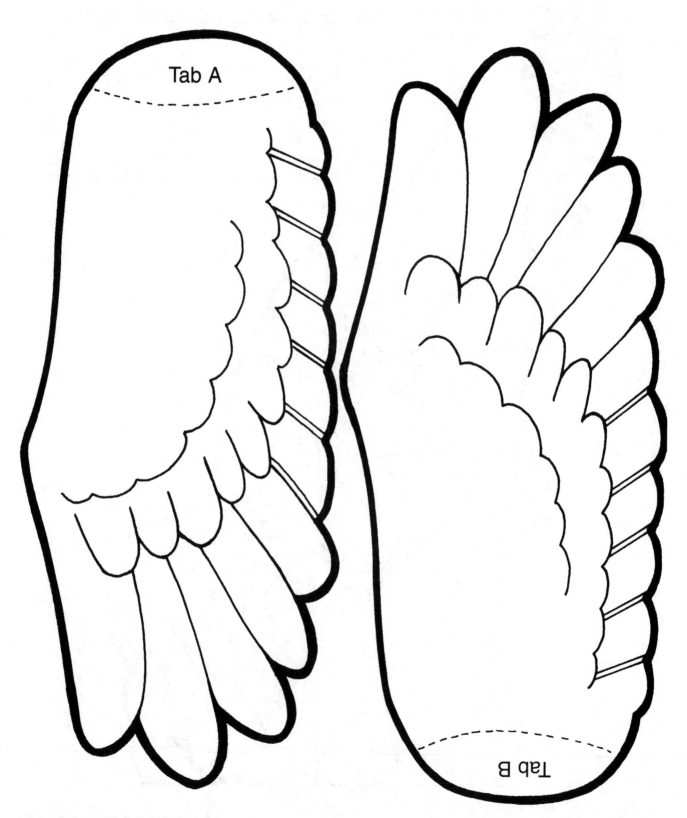

Tab A

Tab B

Statue of Liberty

Use pages 271–273. Cut out the three sections of the Statue of Liberty. Attach torso at Tab A. Connect pedestal at Tab B. Color and display statue.

Tab A

Statue of Liberty *(cont.)*

Statue of Liberty (cont.)

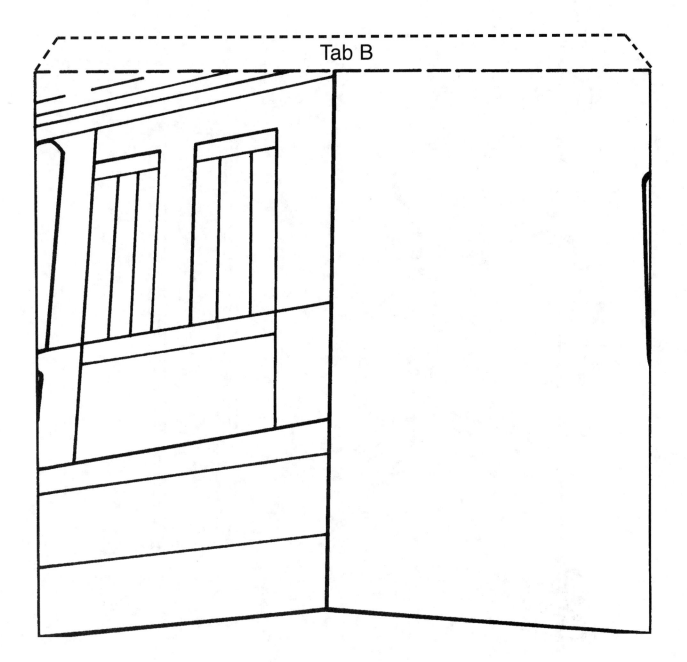

Tab B

Liberty Bell

Use pages 274–275. Cut out and connect at the tab.

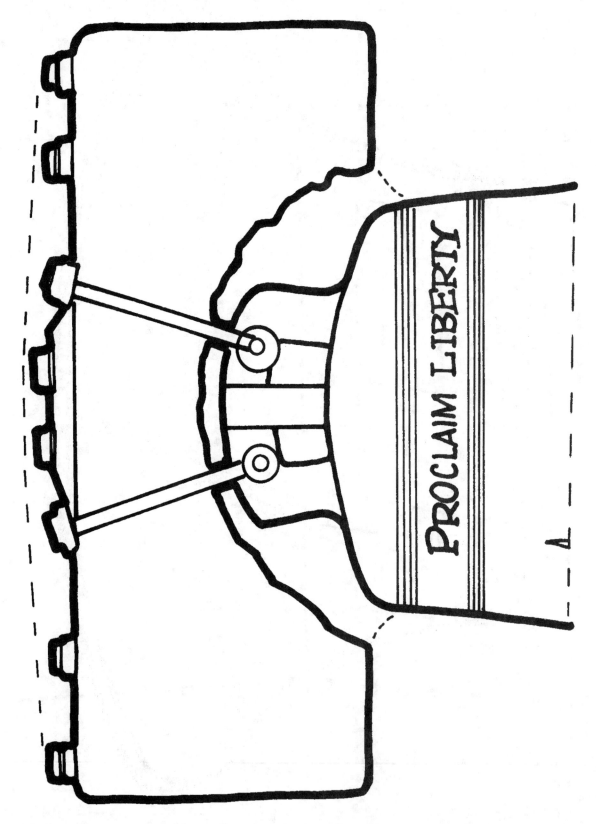

PROCLAIM LIBERTY

Liberty Bell (cont.)

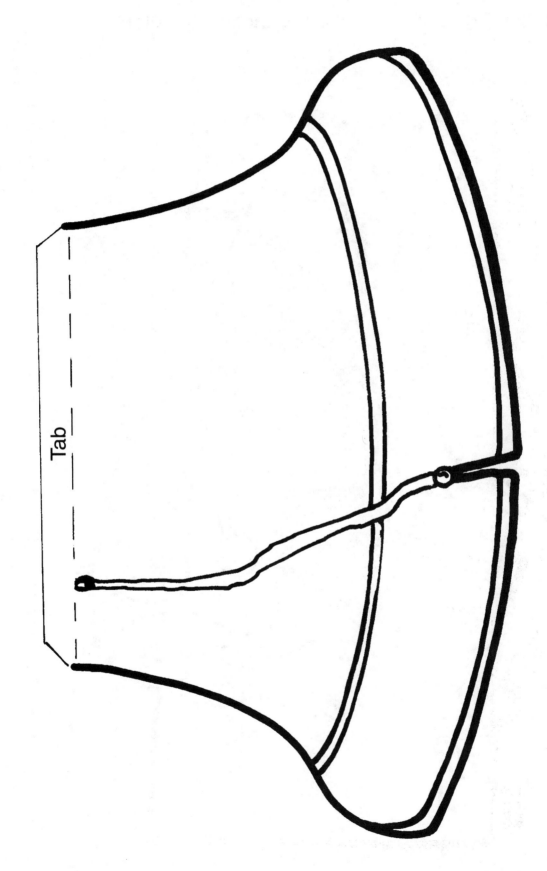

Tab

Doctor

Use pages 276-277. Cut out and connect at the tab.

Doctor *(cont.)*

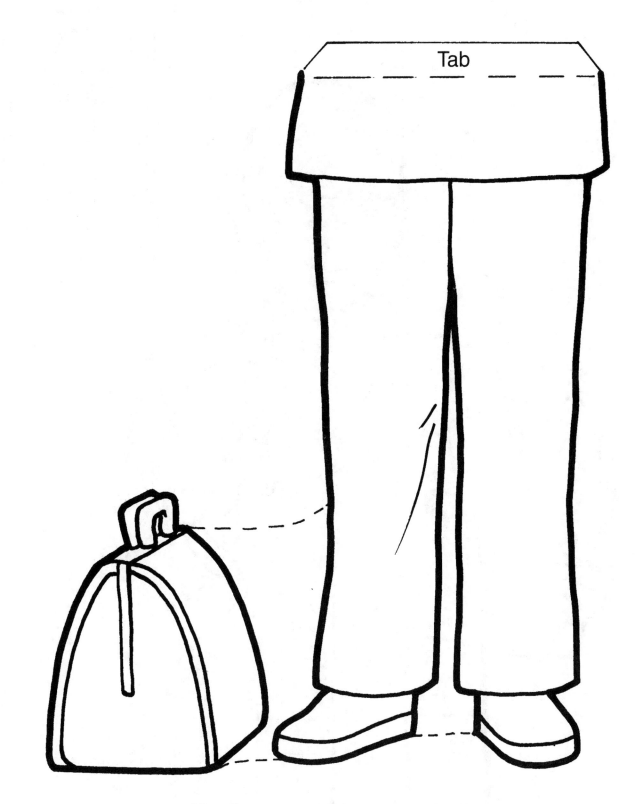

Tab

Dentist

Use pages 278–279. Cut out and connect at the tab.

Dentist *(cont.)*

Tab

Mail Carrier

Use pages 280–281. Cut out mail carrier and connect at Tab A. Attach mailbag at Tab B (behind elbow).

Tab A

Mail Carrier *(cont.)*

Tab B

Police Officer

Use pages 282–283. Cut out and connect at the tab.

Police Officer *(cont.)*

Tab

Firefighter

Use pages 284–285.

Cut out the firefighter and connect at the tab.
Use hydrant on page 286.

Tab

Firefighter (cont.)

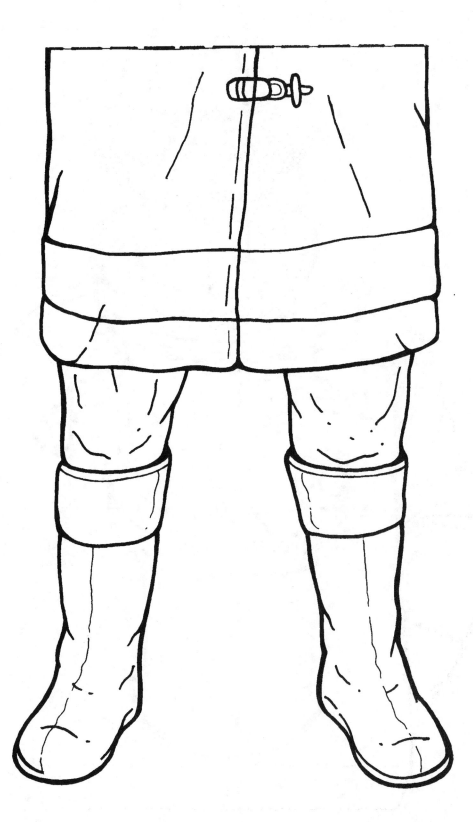

Fire Hydrant

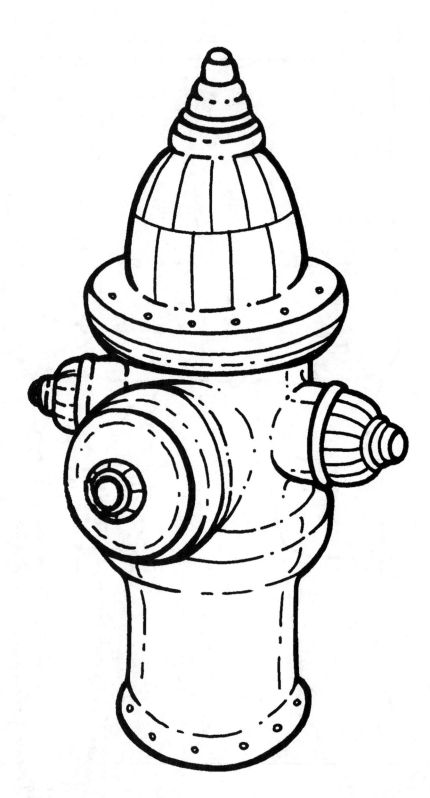

286

Teacher

Social Studies

Use pages 287–288. Cut out the teacher and connect at the tab.

Teacher *(cont.)*

Tab

288

Car

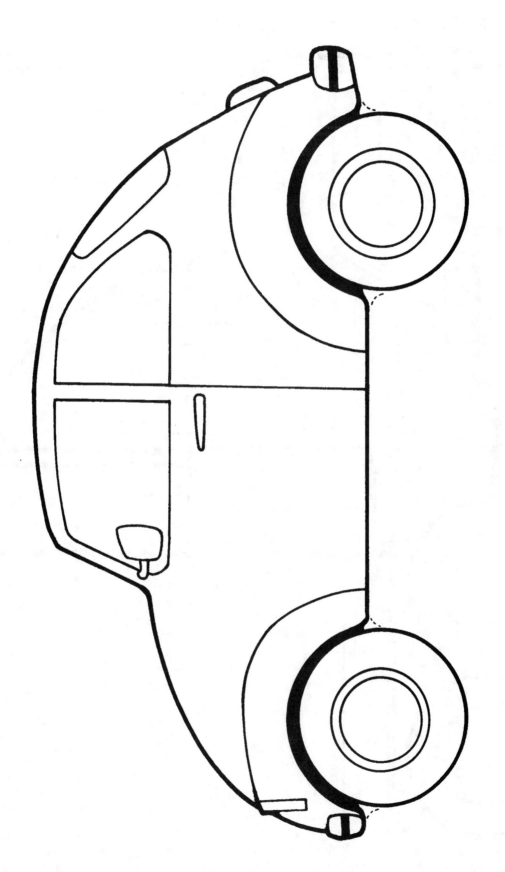

Truck

Use pages 290–291. Cut out and connect at the tab.

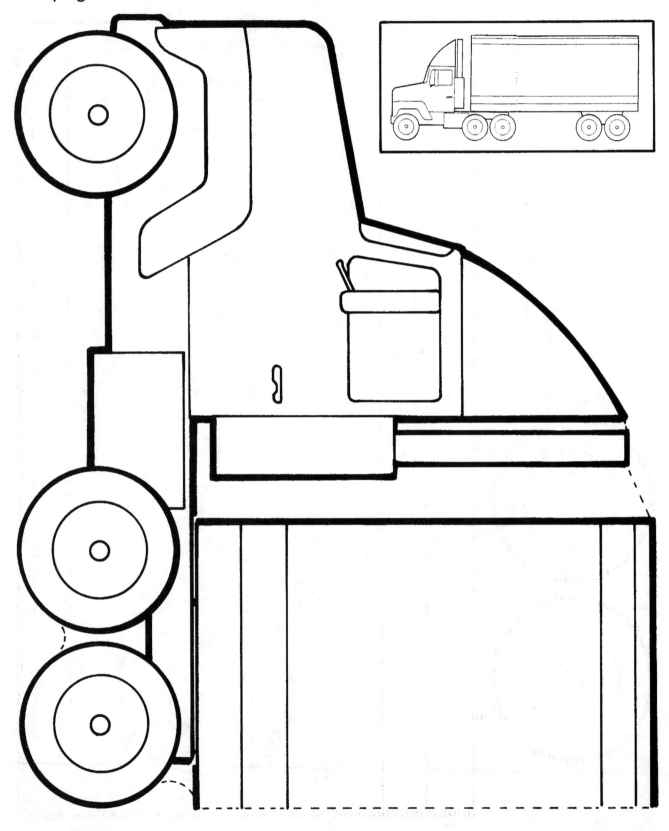

Truck *(cont.)*

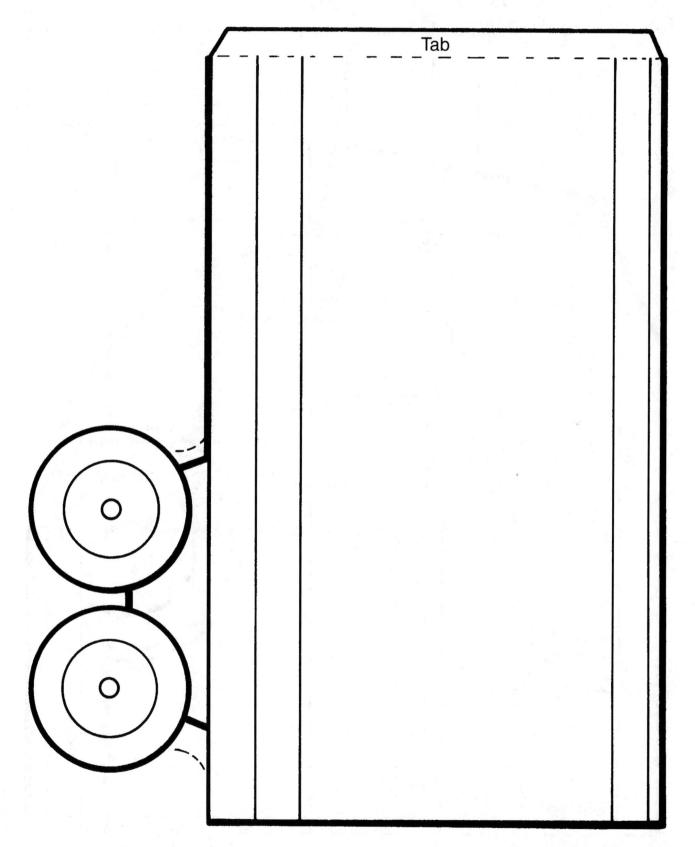

Tab

Bus

Use pages 292–293.
Connect the bus at the tab.

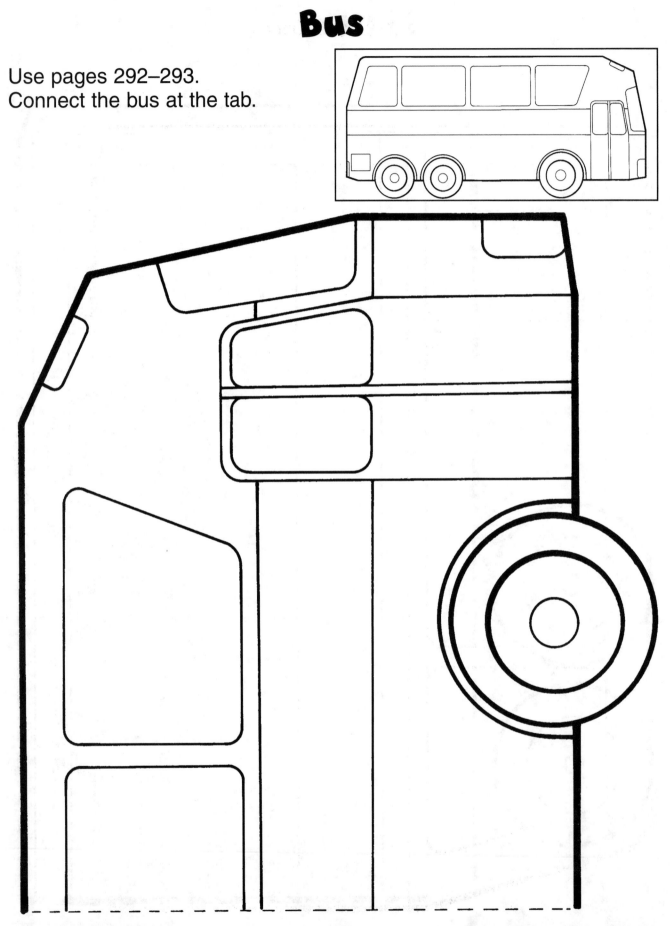

292   © Teacher Created Materials, Inc.

Bus *(cont.)*

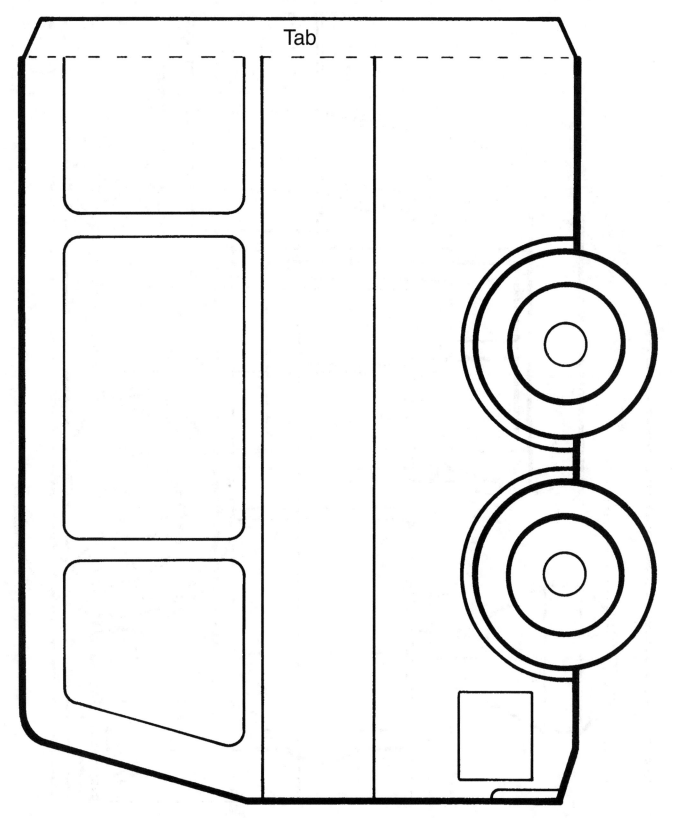

Tab

Train

Use pages 294–296. Connect the engine to the boxcar at Tab A.
Connect the caboose to the boxcar at Tab B.

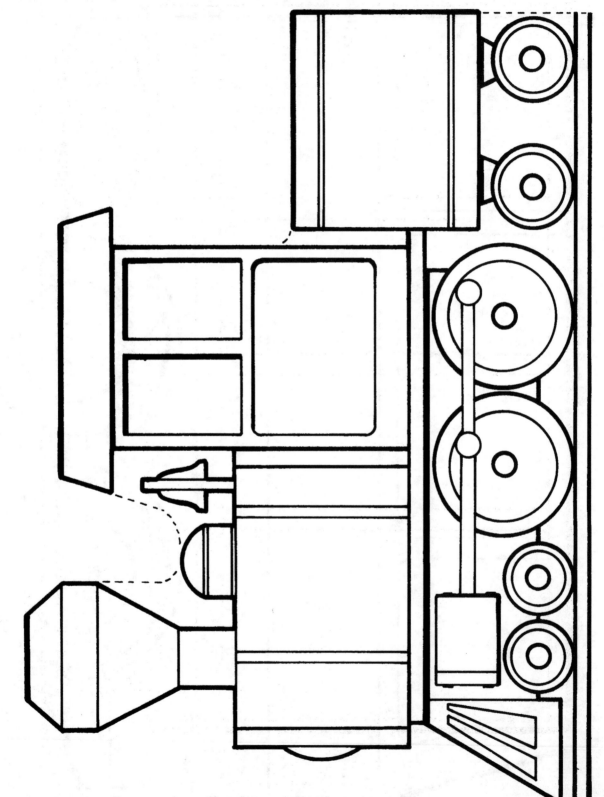

Train *(cont.)*

Tab A

Train (cont.)

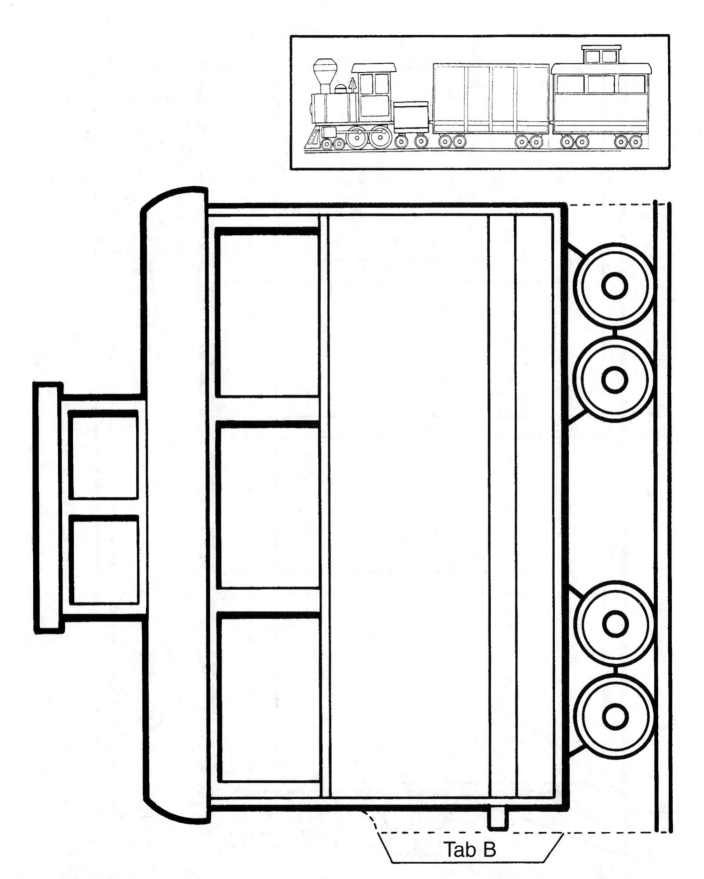

Tab B

Airplane

Use pages 297–298. See diagram for wing placement.

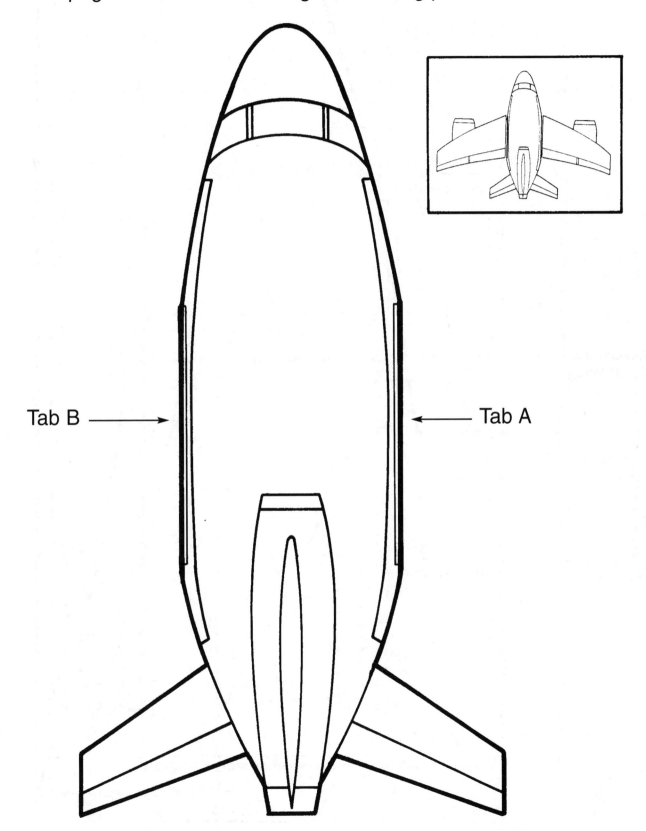

Tab B

Tab A

Airplane *(cont.)*

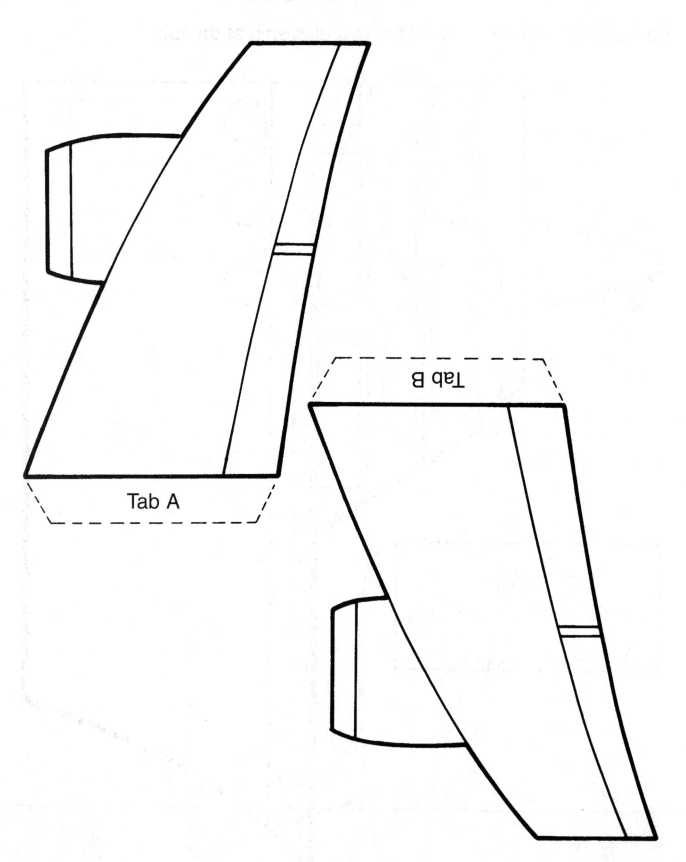

Tab A

Tab B

Cruise Ship

Use pages 299–300. Connect the cruise ship at the tab.

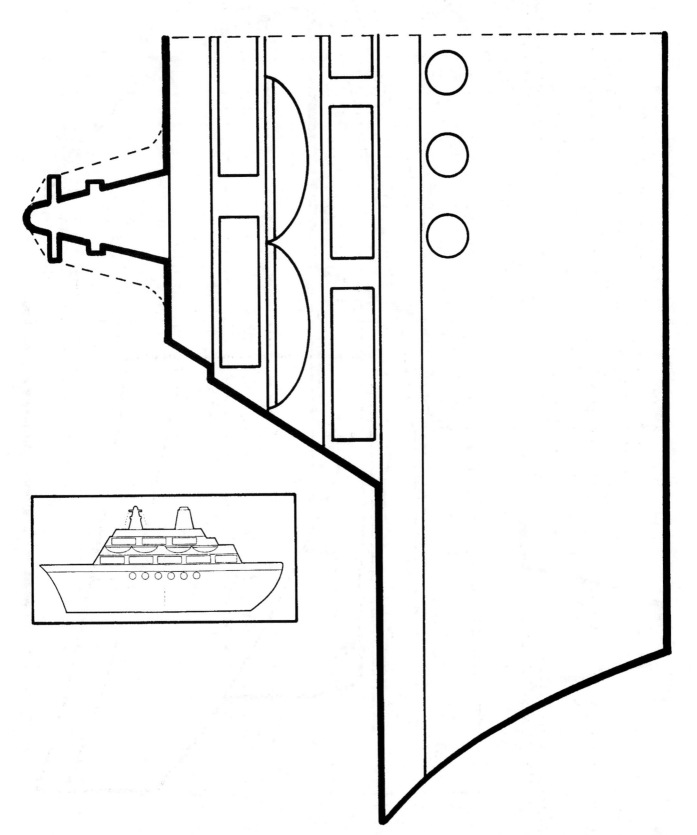

Cruise Ship (cont.)

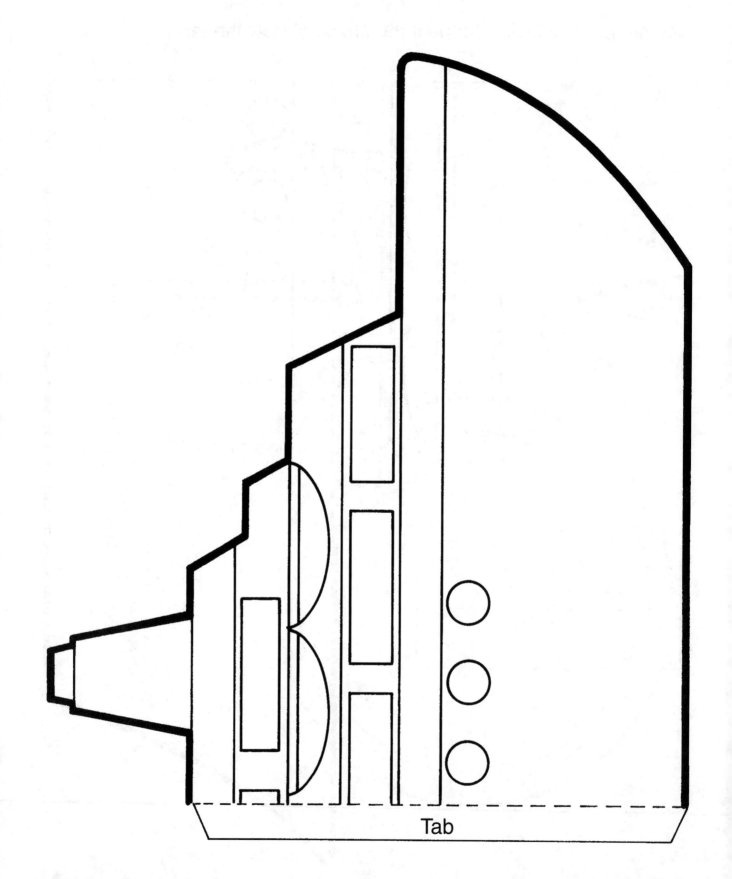

Tab

Bicycle

Use pages 301–302. Connect the bike at the tab.

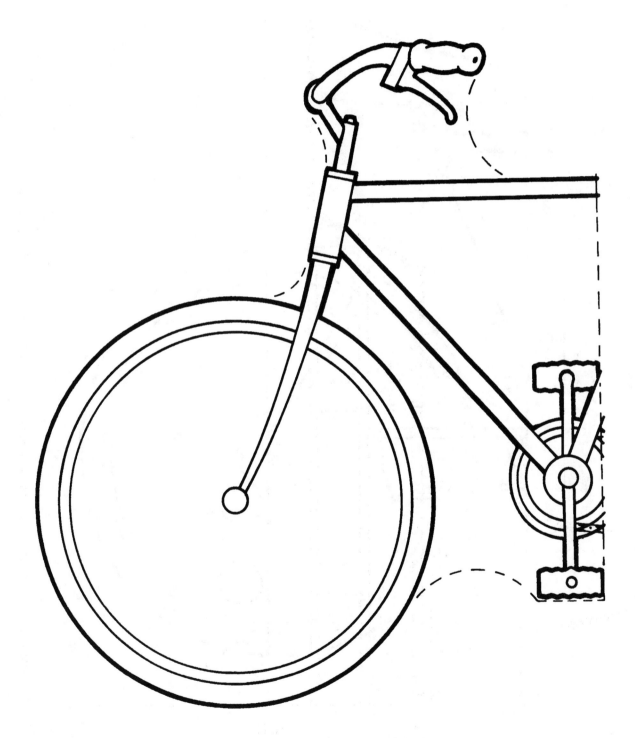

Bicycle *(cont.)*

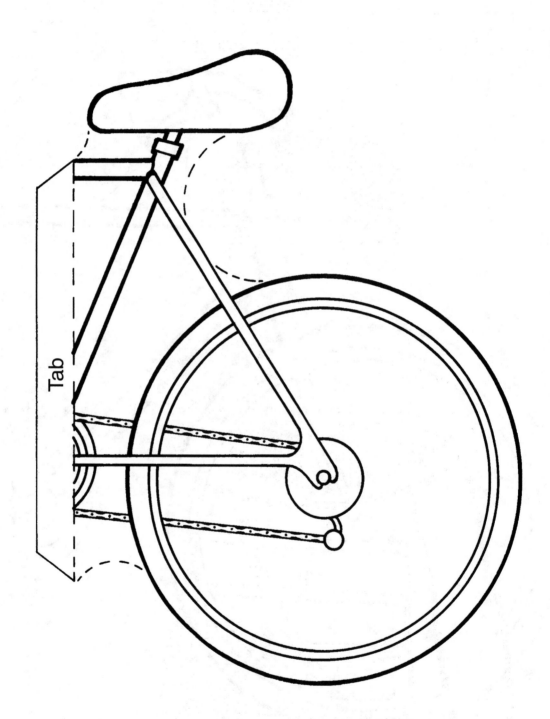

Tab

302

Clothing and Costumes
of the World

Tanzania

Use pages 303–304. Cut out and connect at the tab.

Clothing and Costumes
of the World *(cont.)*

Tanzania

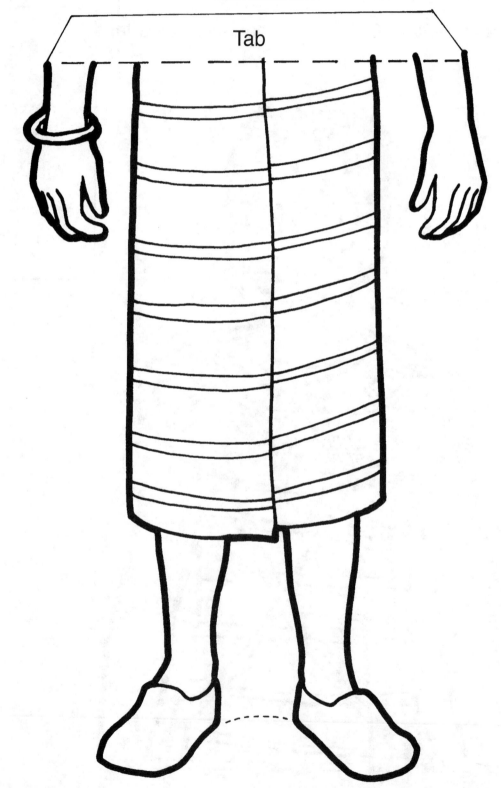

Tab

Clothing and Costumes
of the World *(cont.)*

Japan

Use pages 305–306.

Cut out and connect
at the tab.

Clothing and Costumes
of the World *(cont.)*

Japan

Tab

Clothing and Costumes
of the World (cont.)

Argentina

Use pages 307–308. Cut out and connect at the tab.

Clothing and Costumes of the World *(cont.)*

Argentina

Tab

Clothing and Costumes
of the World *(cont.)*

Holland

Use pages 309–310. Cut out and connect at the tab.

Clothing and Costumes
of the World *(cont.)*

Holland

Tab

Clothing and Costumes
of the World *(cont.)*

Australia

Use pages 311–312. Cut out and connect at the tab.

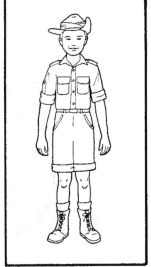

Clothing and Costumes
of the World *(cont.)*

Australia

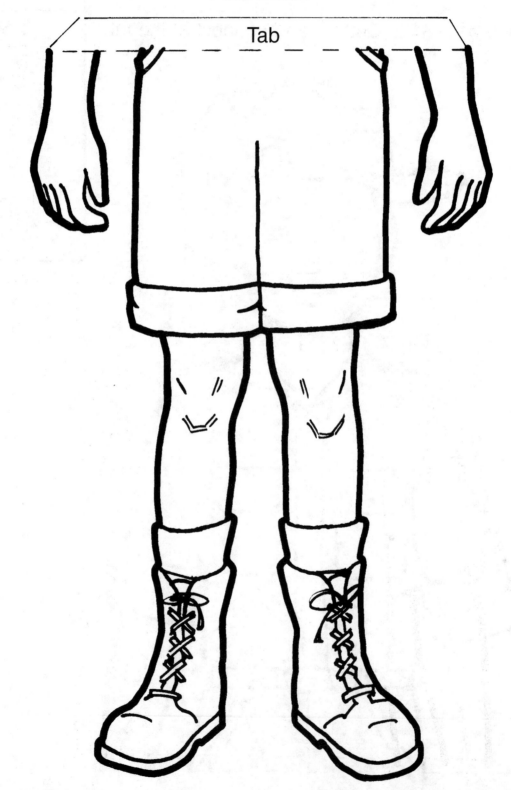

Tab

Clothing and Costumes
of the World *(cont.)*

Play Clothes

Use pages 313–314. Cut out and connect at the tab.

Play Clothes *(cont.)*

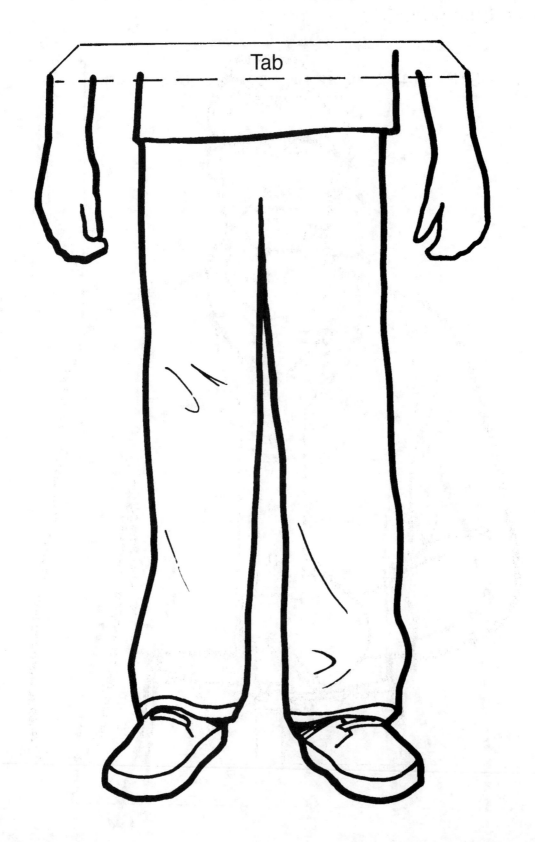

Tab

Cowboy

Use pages 315–317. Cut out and connect at the tab. Add the hat and the lasso from page 317.

Cowboy *(cont.)*

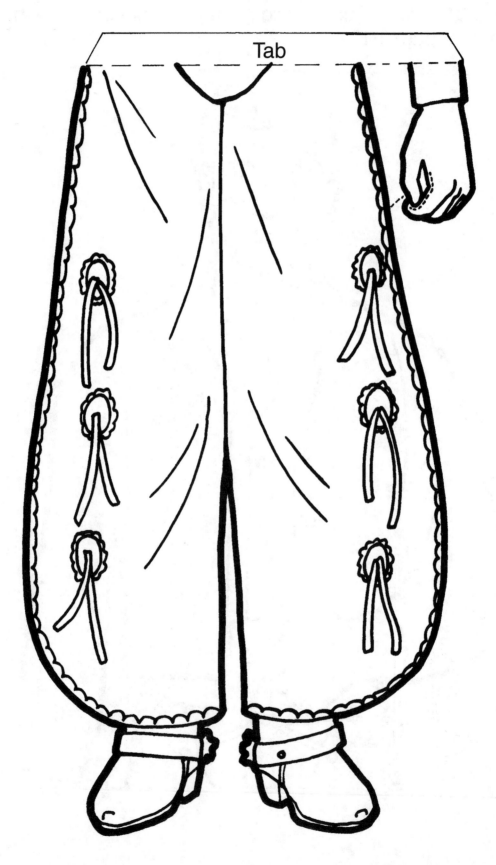

Tab

Cowboy *(cont.)*

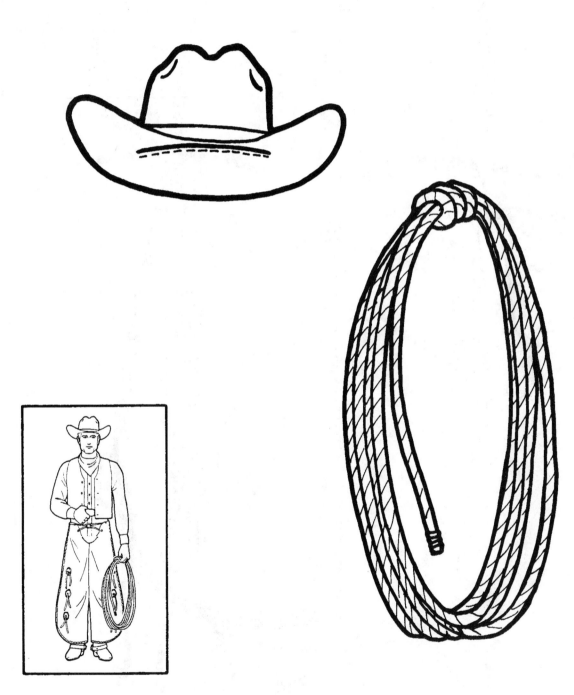

Longhorn Steer

Use pages 318–319. Connect the steer at the tab.

Longhorn Steer *(cont.)*

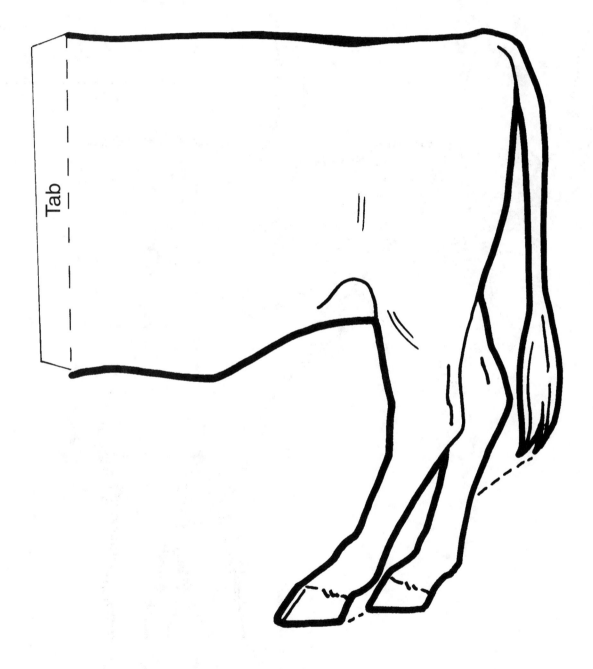

Tab

Horse

Use pages 320–321. Connect the horse at the tab.

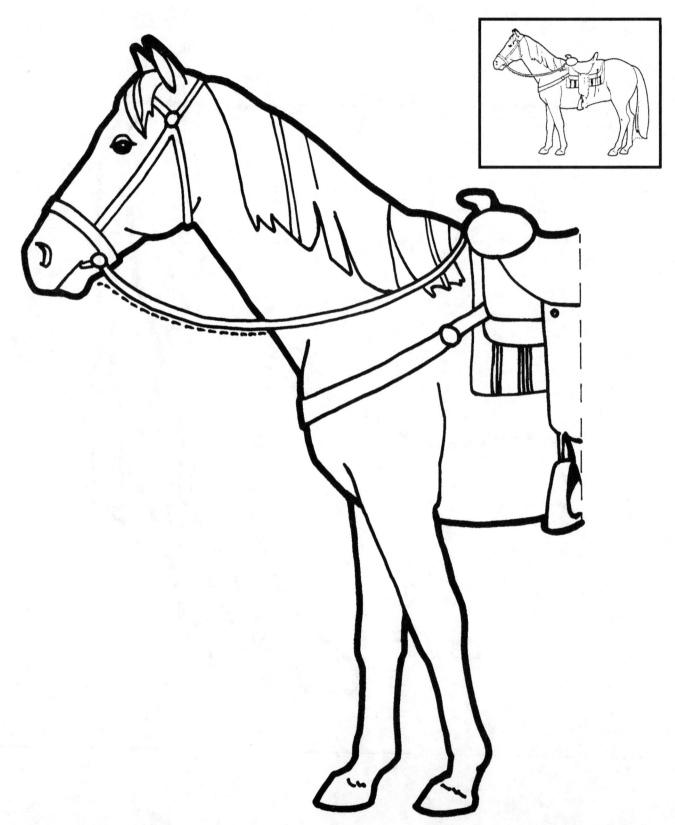

Horse *(cont.)*

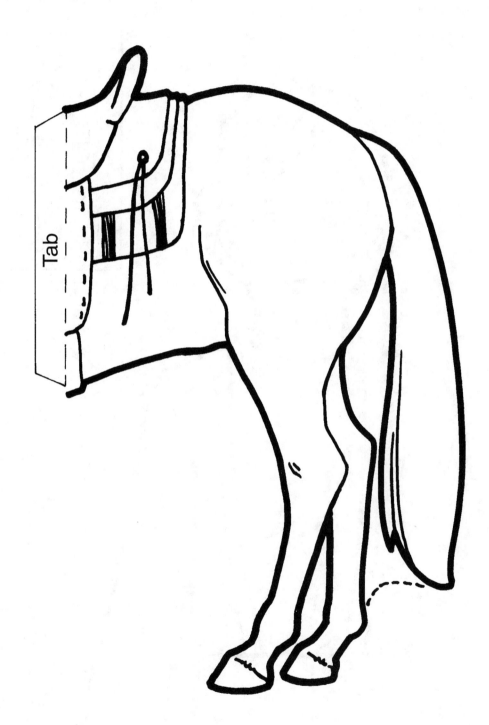

Tab

Pioneer Boy

Use pages 322–323. Connect the boy at the tab.

Pioneer Boy *(cont.)*

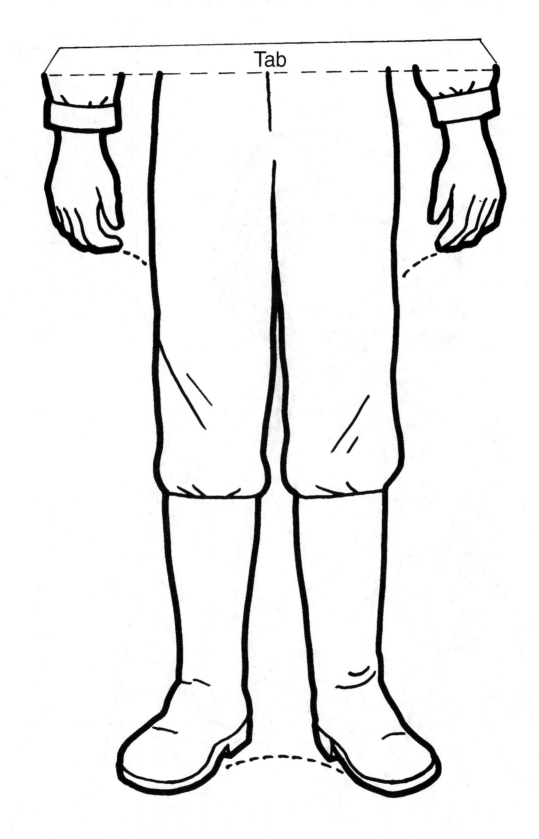

Tab

Pioneer Girl

Use pages 324–325. Connect the girl at the tab.

324

Pioneer Girl *(cont.)*

Tab

Covered Wagon

Use pages 326–329.
See directions on page 327.

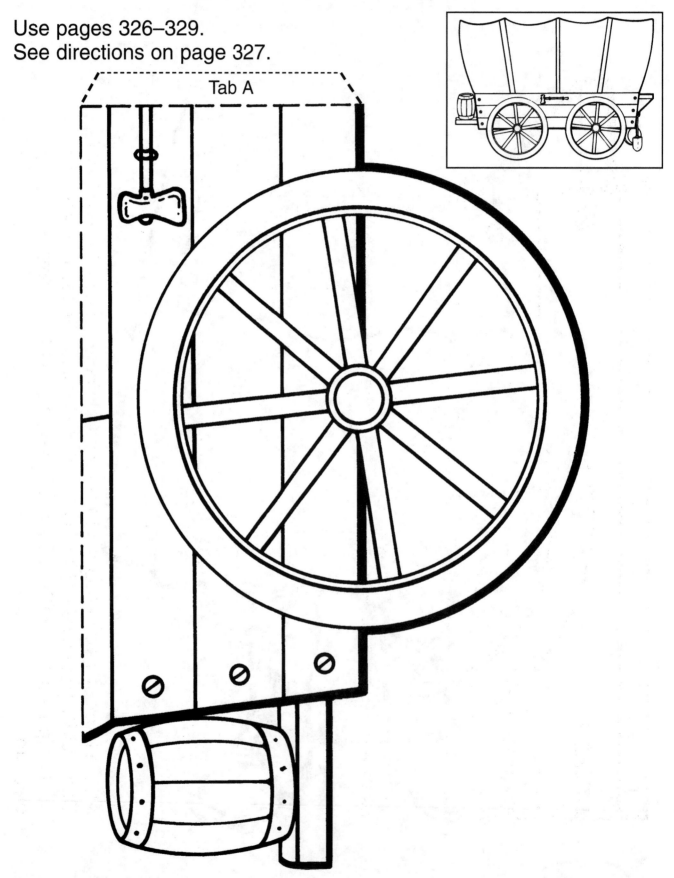

Tab A

Covered Wagon *(cont.)*

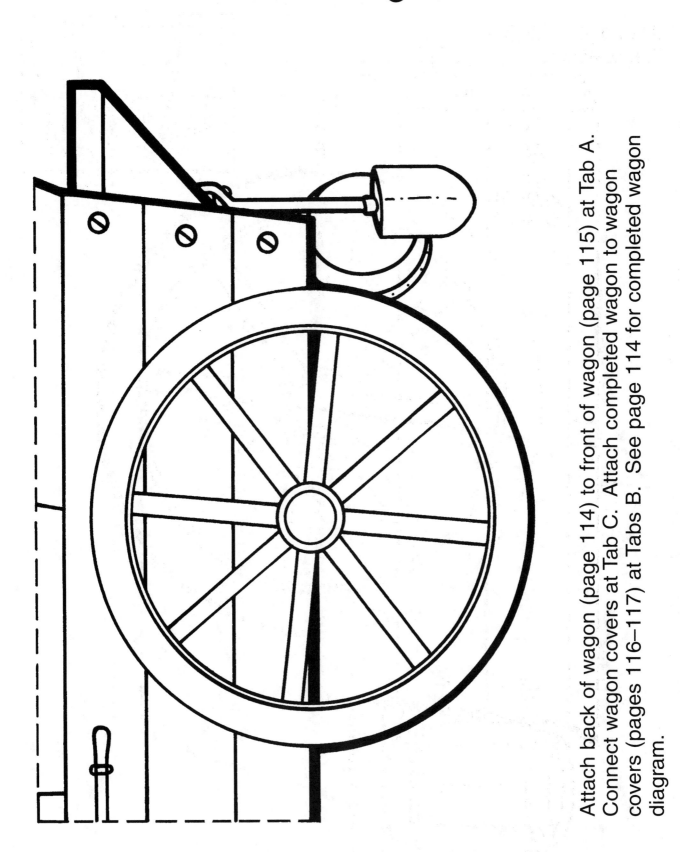

Attach back of wagon (page 114) to front of wagon (page 115) at Tab A. Connect wagon covers at Tab C. Attach completed wagon to wagon covers (pages 116–117) at Tabs B. See page 114 for completed wagon diagram.

Covered Wagon *(cont.)*

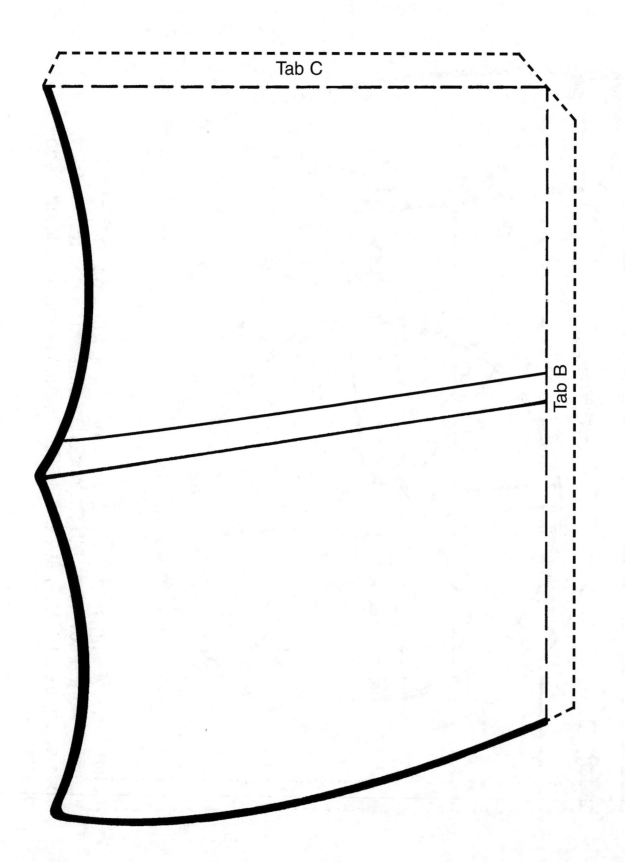

Tab C

Tab B

Covered Wagon *(cont.)*

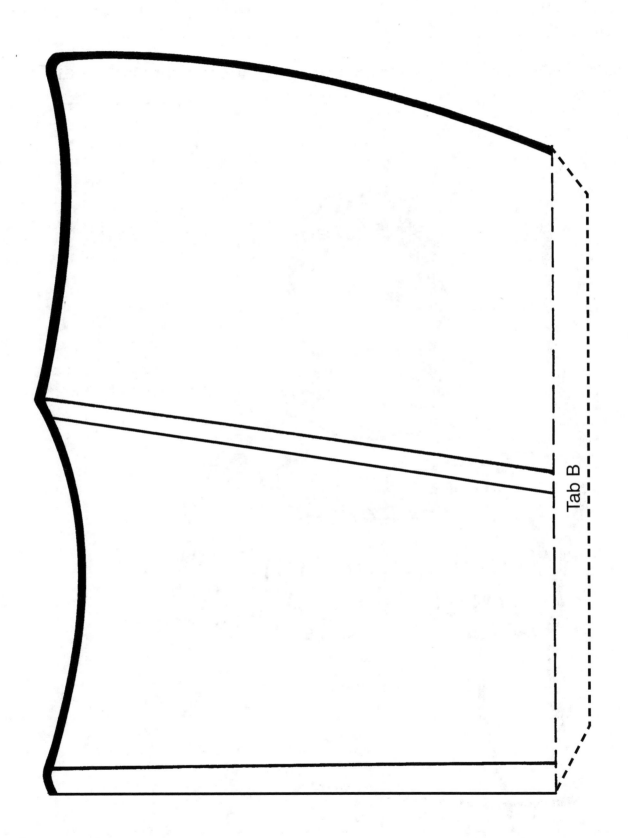

Tab B

Iroquois Female and Infant

The Iroquois people are from the northeastern region of the United States.

Use pages 330-332. Connect torso at Tab A. Attach arms at Tabs B and C.

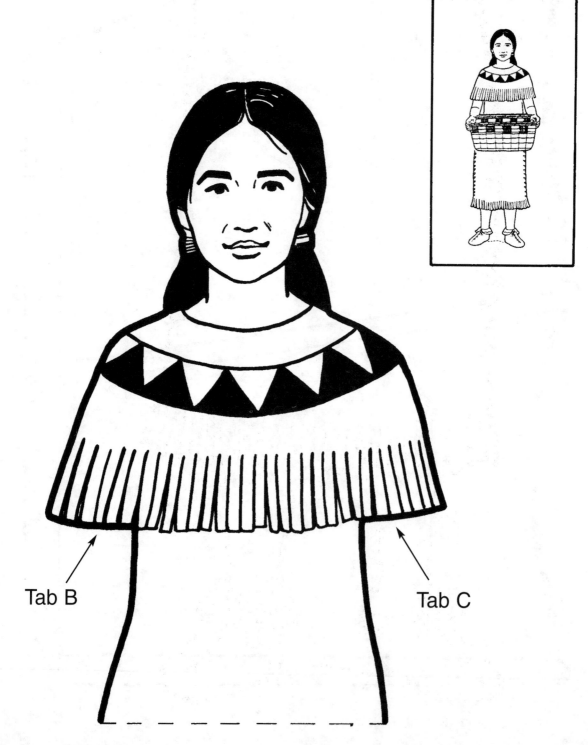

Tab B

Tab C

330

Iroquois Female and Infant *(cont.)*

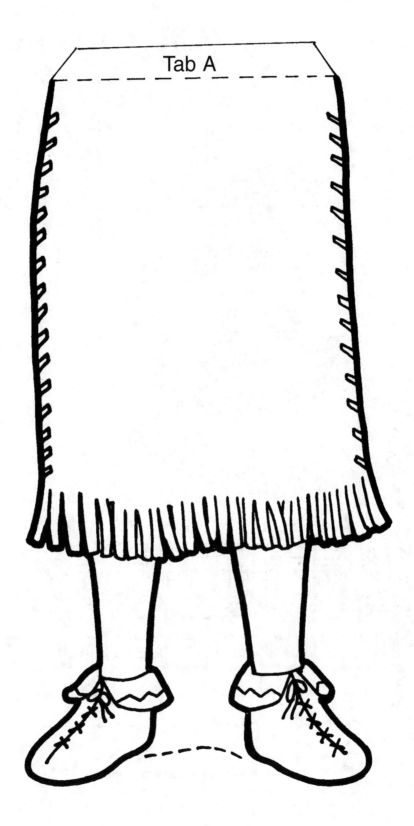

Iroquois Female and Infant *(cont.)*

Baby in a
Cradle Board

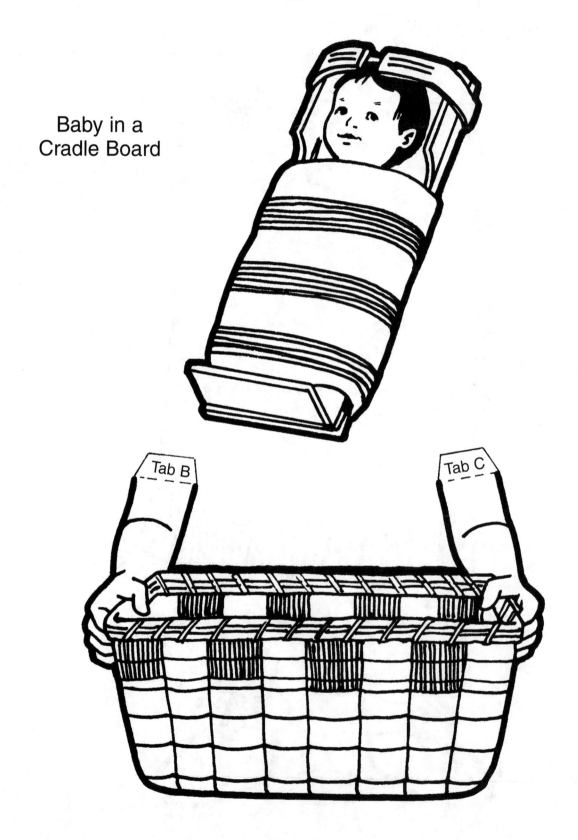

Tab B

Tab C

Iroquois Male

Use pages 333–335. Connect torso at Tab A.
Attach arms at Tabs B and C.

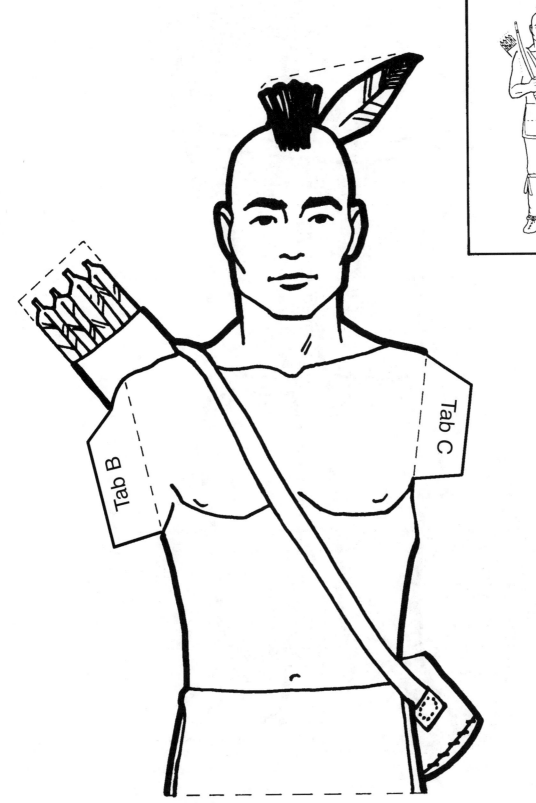

Tab B

Tab C

Iroquois Male *(cont.)*

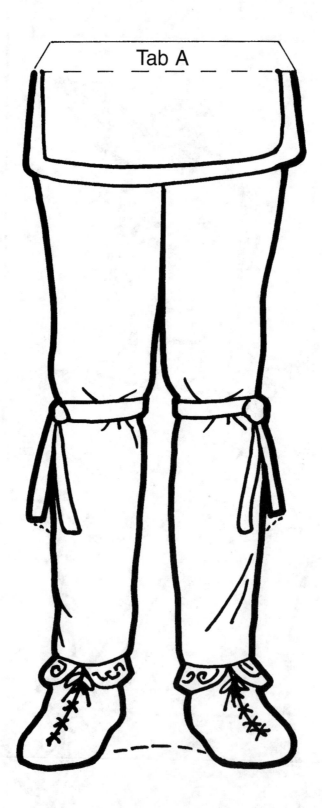

Tab A

Iroquois Male *(cont.)*

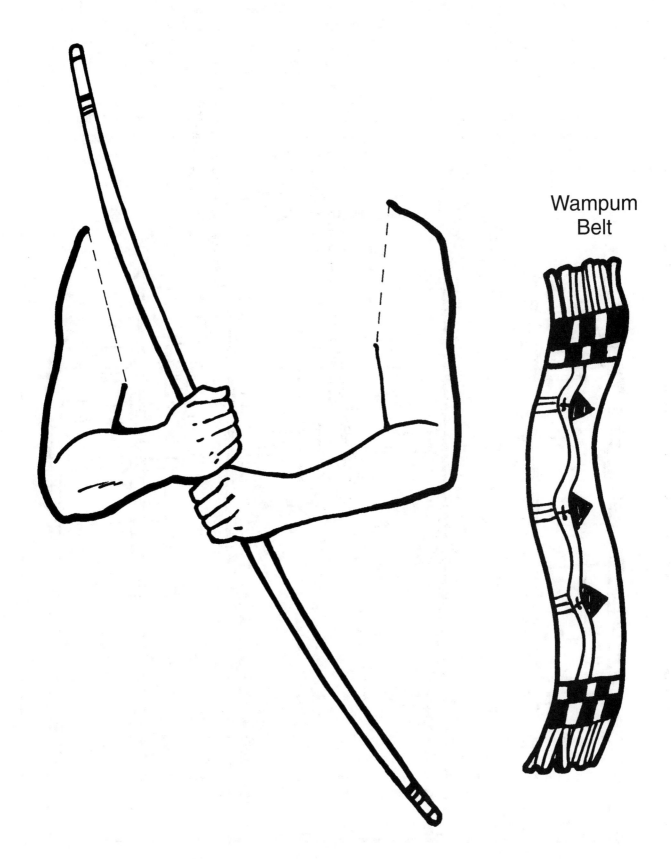

Wampum
Belt

Long House

The Iroquois of the Northeast lived in large, rectangular houses that had slanted or rounded roofs made of wood. Use pages 336–339 to create a paper model of a long house. Follow the directions for each section located at the top of each page. When completed, the long house will be 6" x 15" x 7". For best results, use sturdy paper. See picture of completed house on page 338.

Front and Back—Make two copies of page 336. One copy will be the front of the house, and the second copy will be the back of the house. Color and cut out the front and back of the house. Connect the front and back of the house to the walls at Tabs F. Connect Tabs A to the roof.

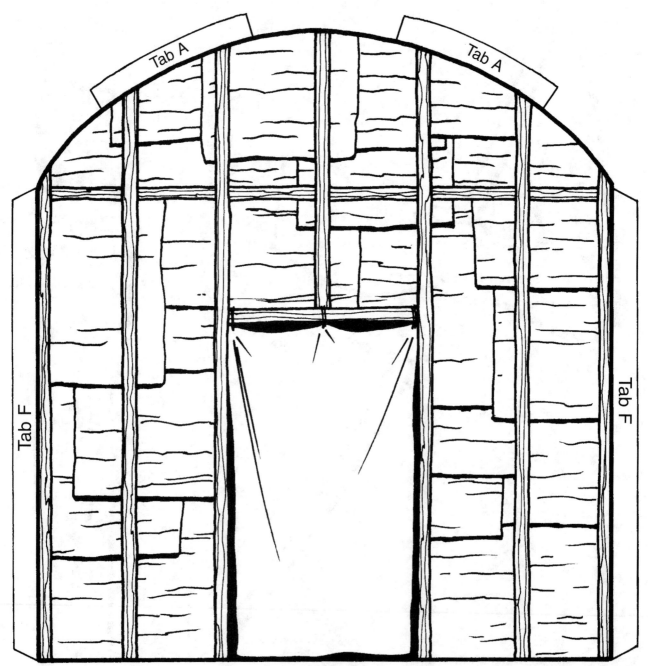

Long House *(cont.)*

Walls—Make four copies of the wall. Color and cut out each wall. Tape or glue two walls at Tab B to form one long wall. Cut off the other Tab B. Repeat for the other two walls. Connect each wall section to Tabs F located on the front and back section of the house.

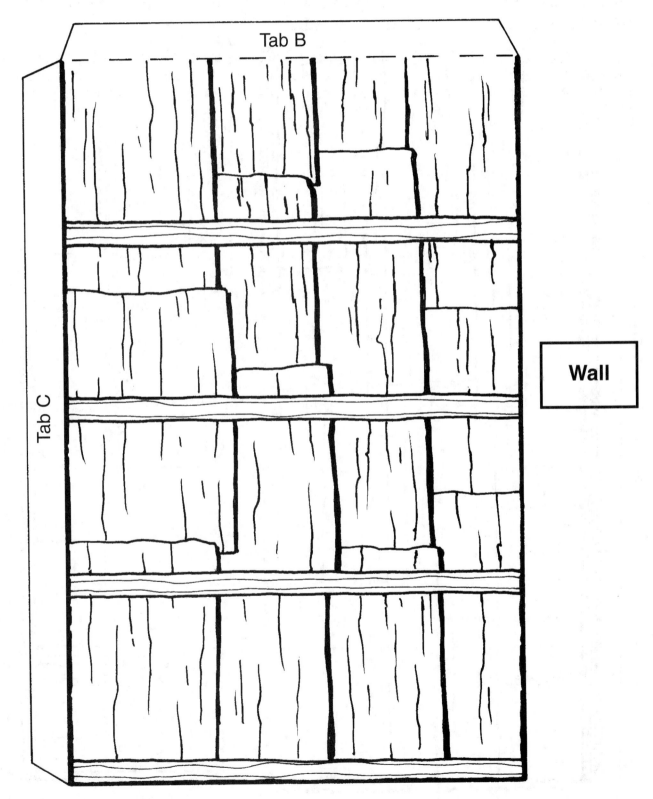

Tab B

Tab C

Wall

Long House *(cont.)*

Roof—Make two copies of page 338. Color and cut out pattern. Cut off one Tab D. Next, align Tab E on each section of the roof. Tape or glue the roofs together along the remaining Tab D. Connect section at Tab E to the other part of roof on page 339.

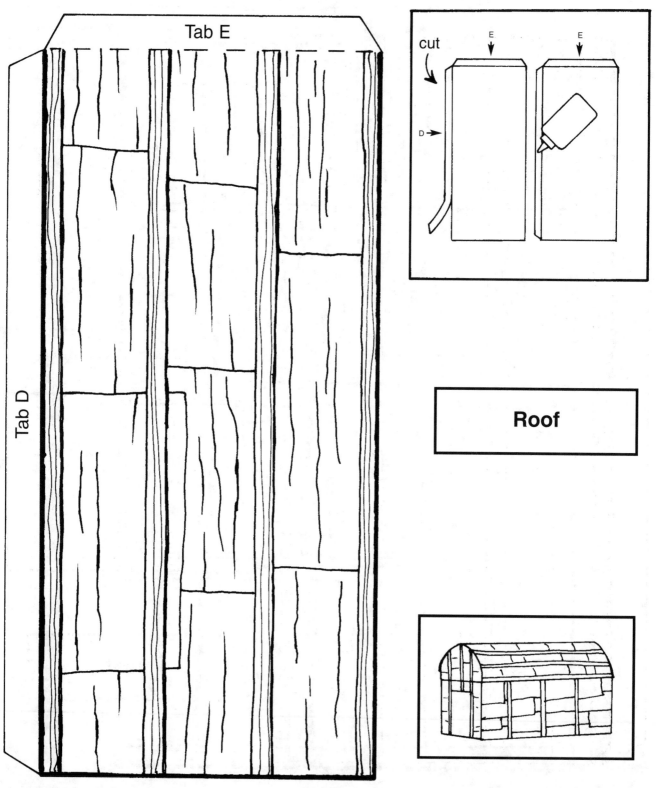

Roof

Long House *(cont.)*

Roof (cont.)—Make two copies of page 339. Color and cut out pattern. Cut off one Tab D. Tape or glue the roofs together along the remaining Tab D. Combine roof sections at Tab E. Attach the complete roof to the walls at Tabs C and to the front and back section of the house at Tabs A.

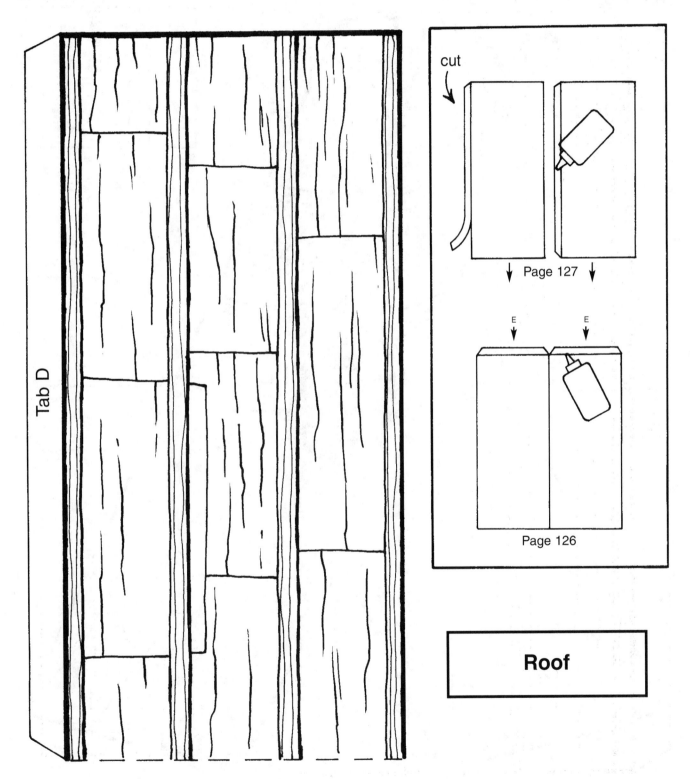

cut

Page 127

E   E

Page 126

Roof

Tipi

Use pages 340–341.

The tipi was constructed from buffalo hides and used by the Plains people.

Color, then tape or glue the two halves together. Then role up in a cone to create a 3–D tipi.

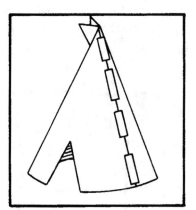

Tipi *(cont.)*

Pueblo

Use pages 342–343.

The people of the Southwest built adobe houses that were joined together like apartment buildings.

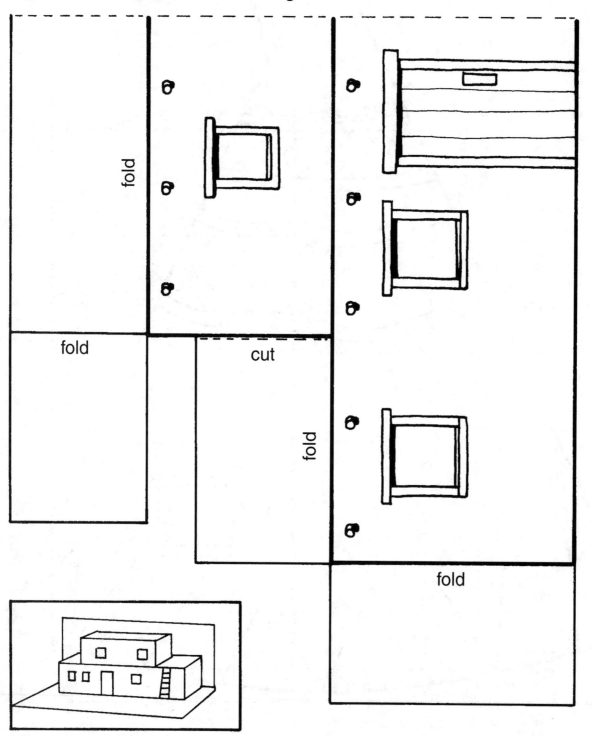

Pueblo *(cont.)*

Cut out and attach two sides of the pueblo at the tab. Fold the pueblo to match the diagram. Attach to a folded piece of tagboard to create back walls.

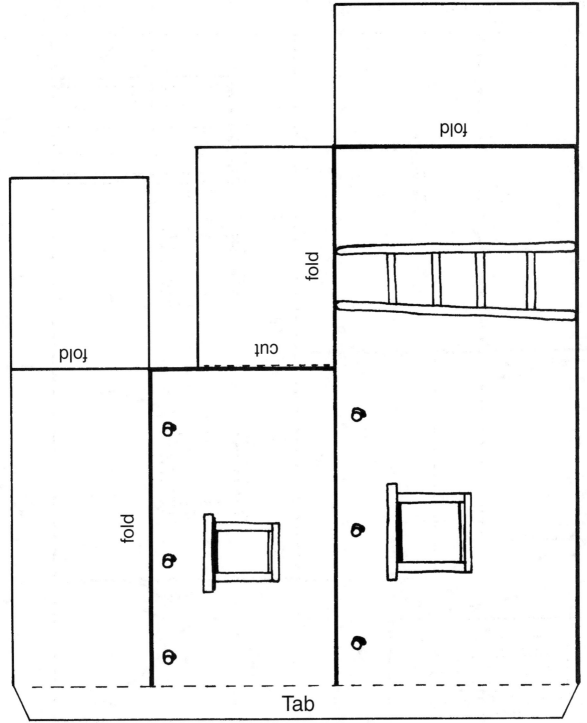

Build a Flower

Use pages 344–345. See diagram for placement of flower parts.

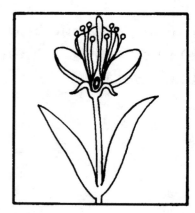

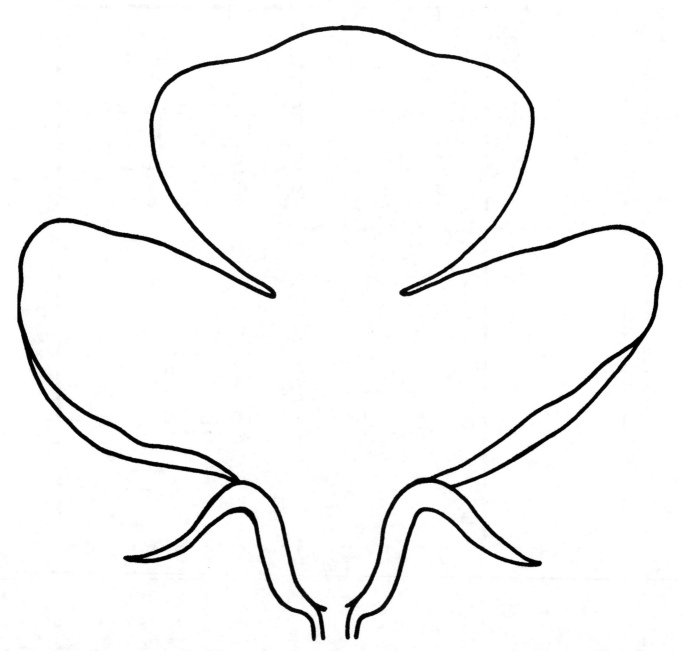

Build a Flower (cont.)

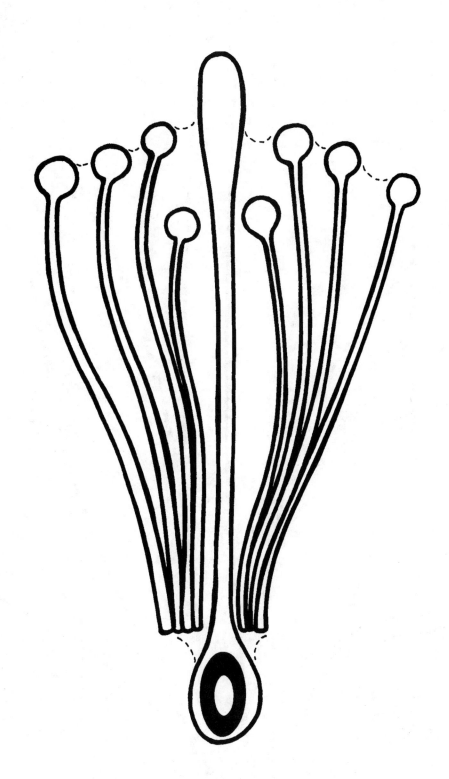

Build a Flower (cont.)

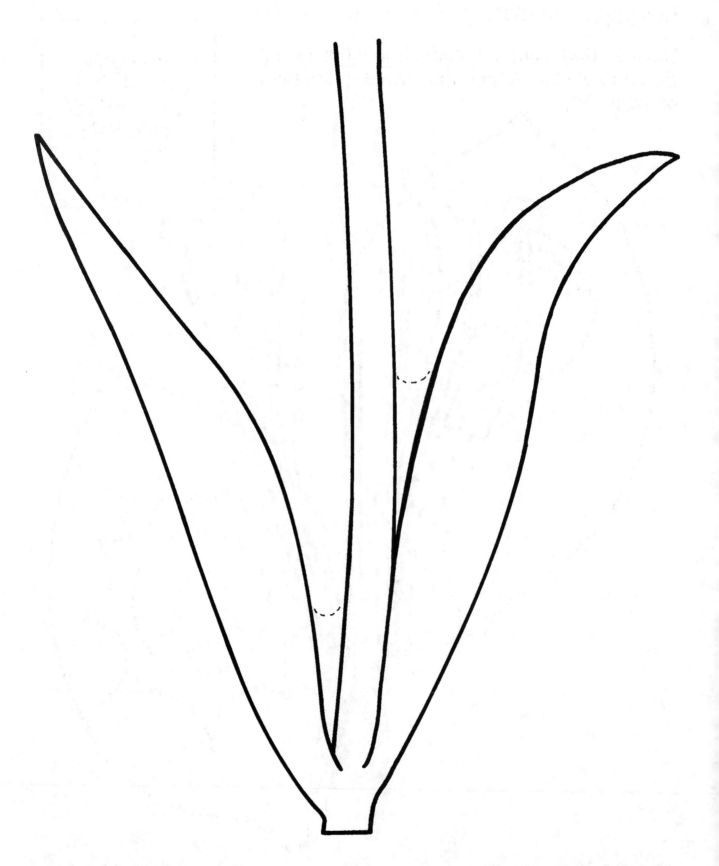

Plant Needs

Use pages 347–349.

Have students cut out, color, and label leaves *Sun* and *Water*. Attach the leaves to the plant on page 349.

Plant Needs *(cont.)*

Have students cut out, color and label leaves *Air* and *Soil*. Attach to the plant on page 349.

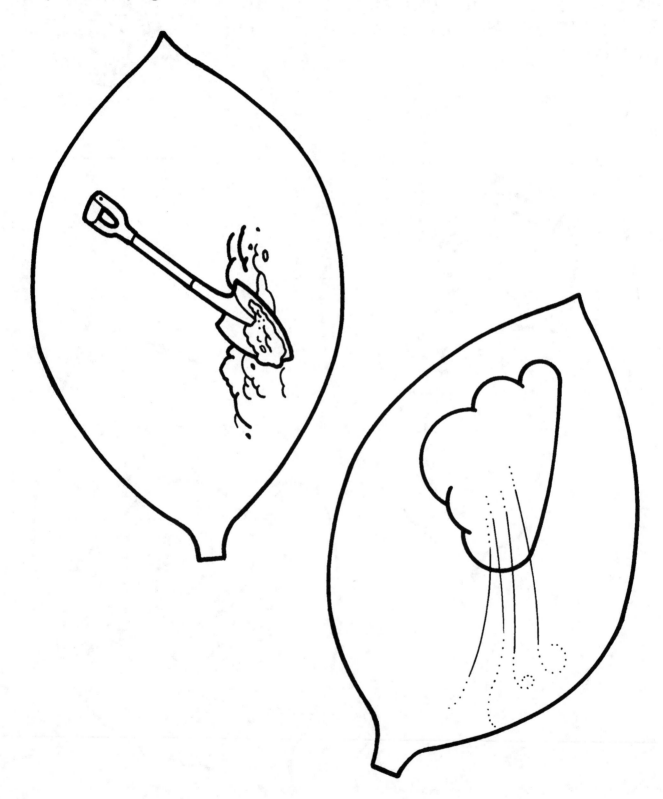

Plant Needs *(cont.)*

Attach the leaves from pages 347–348.

Sun

Wind

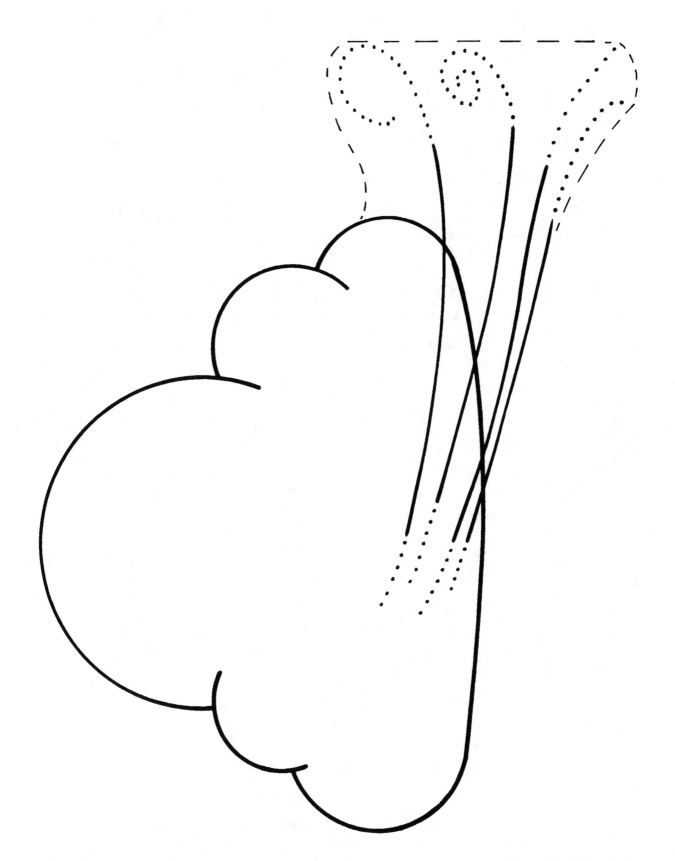

Rain

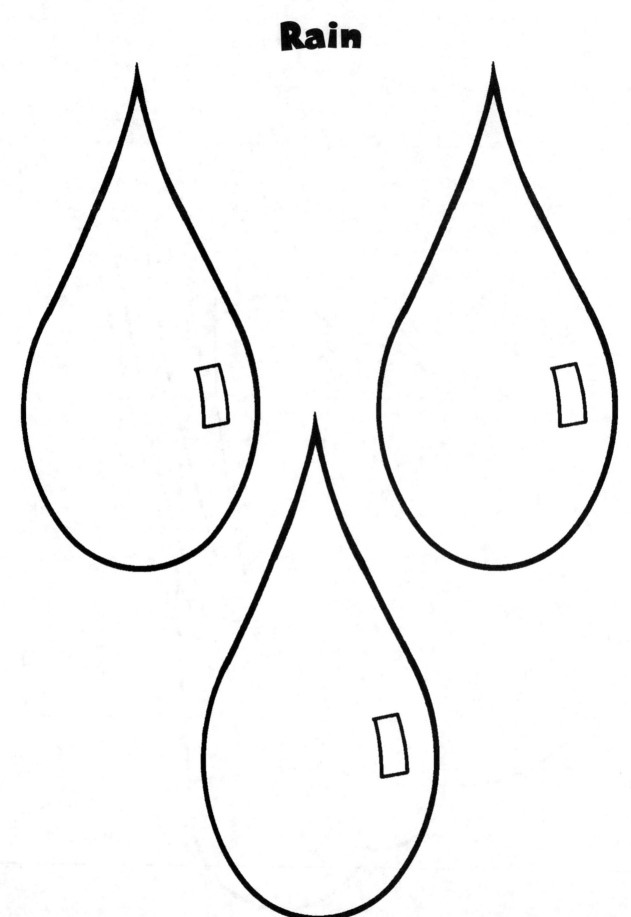

Snowflakes

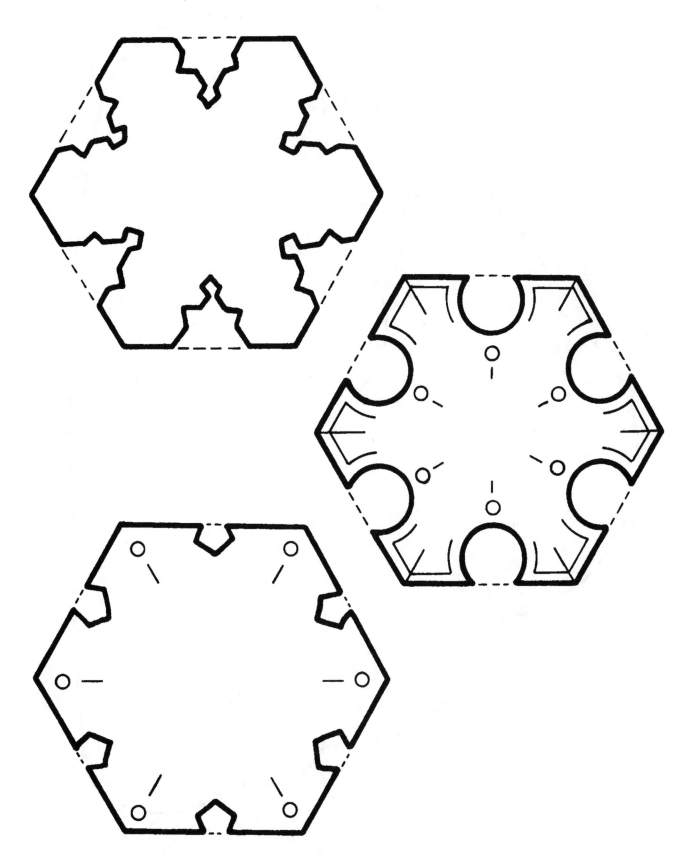

Cloud

354

Rainbow

Use pages 355–356. Connect the rainbow at the tab.

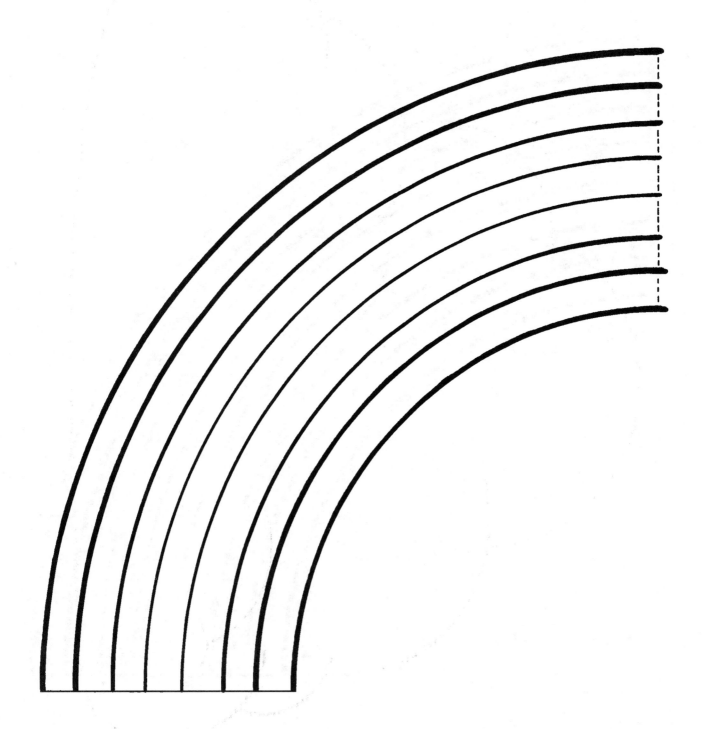

Rainbow *(cont.)*

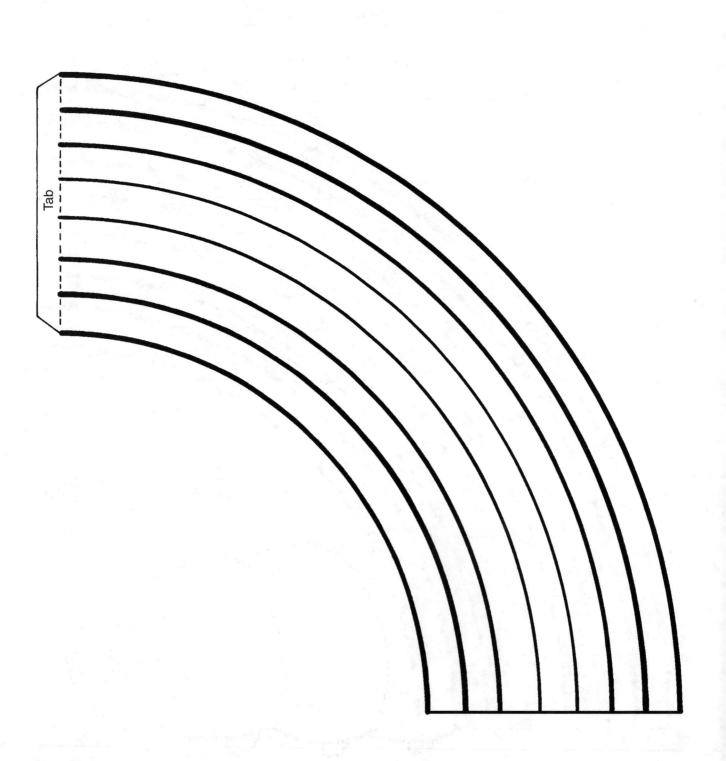

Tab

Stages of a Butterfly

Use pages 357–360.

Eggs

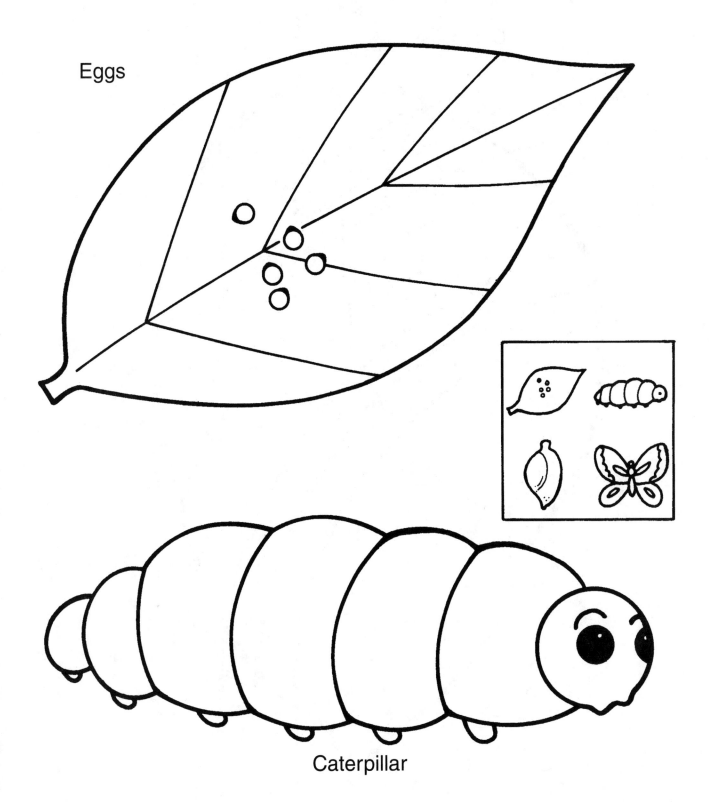

Caterpillar

Stages of a Butterfly (cont.)

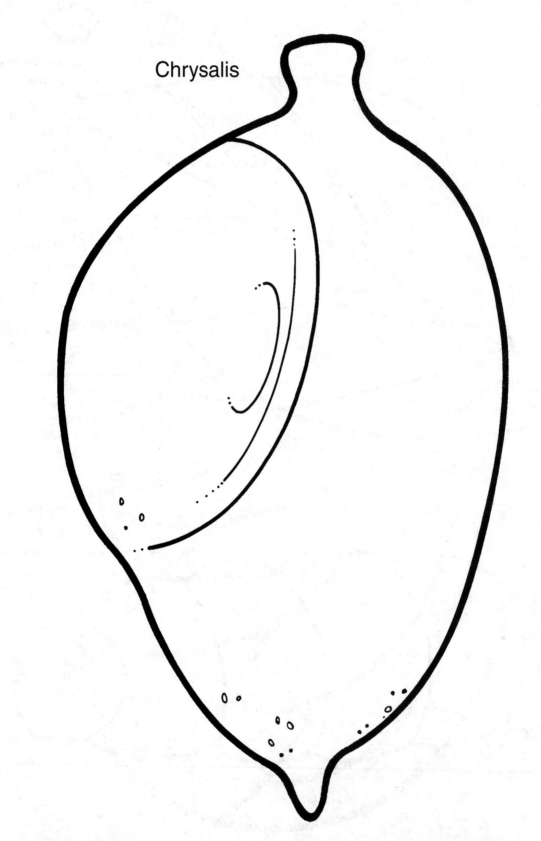

Chrysalis

Stages of a Butterfly (cont.)

Attach body A and right wing by overlapping body A over body B on page 360.

Right Wing

Body

A

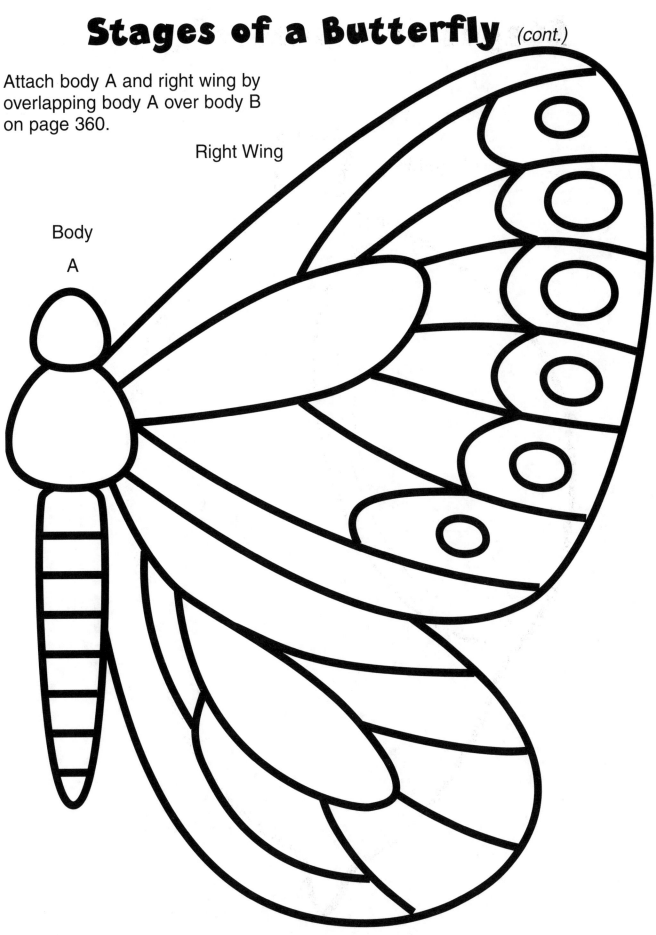

Stages of a Butterfly *(cont.)*

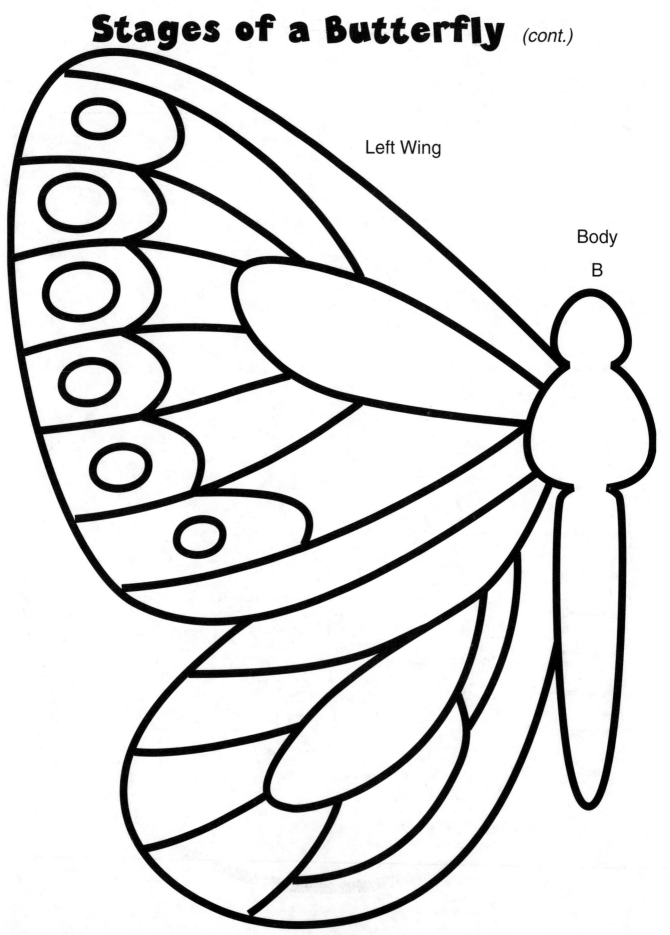

Left Wing

Body

B

Stages of a Frog

Use pages 361–364.

Egg Cluster

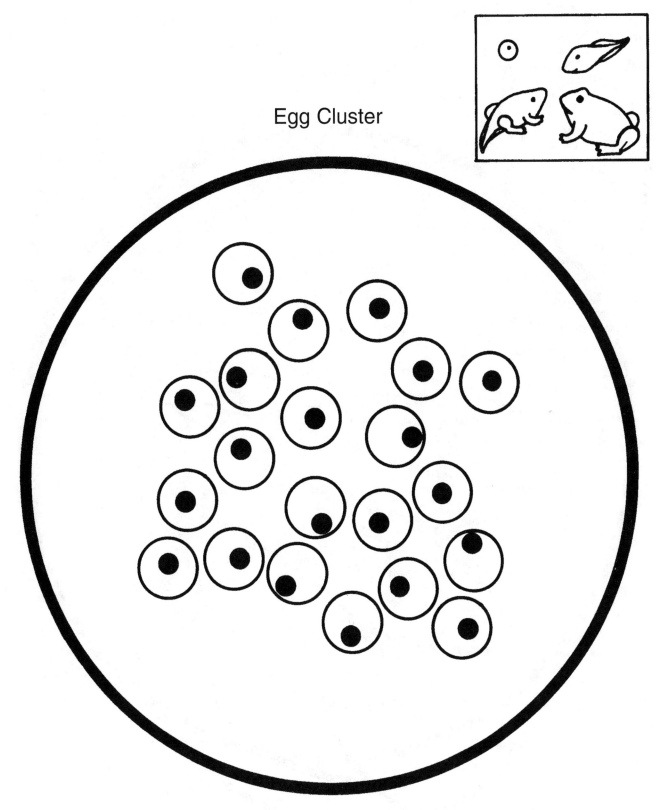

Stages of a Frog *(cont.)*

Tadpole

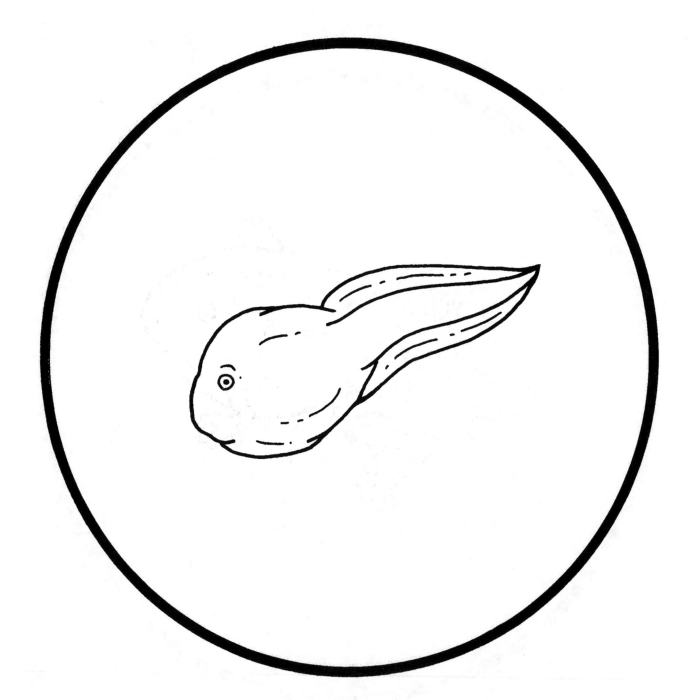

Stages of a Frog *(cont.)*

Tadpole with Emerging Legs

Stages of a Frog *(cont.)*

Frog

364

Tyrannosaurus Rex

Use pages 365–367. Attach head to torso at Tab A. Attach tail to torso at Tab B.

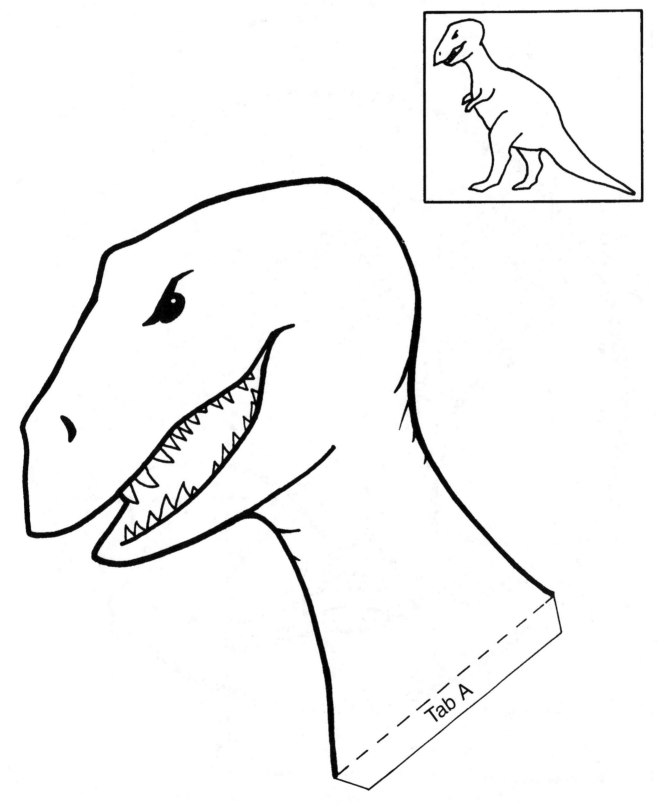

Tab A

Tyrannosaurus Rex (cont.)

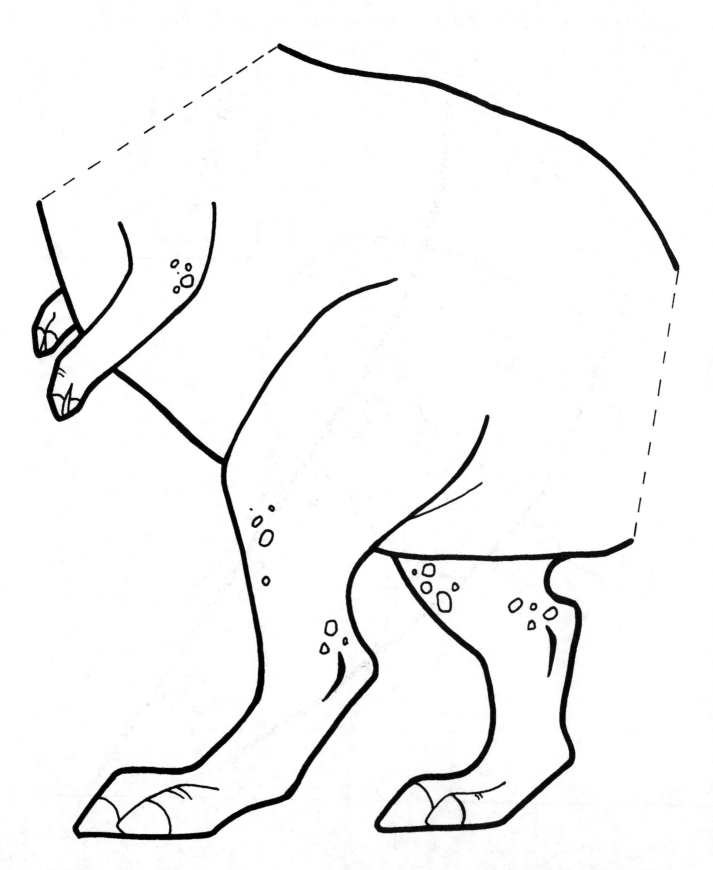

Tyrannosaurus Rex *(cont.)*

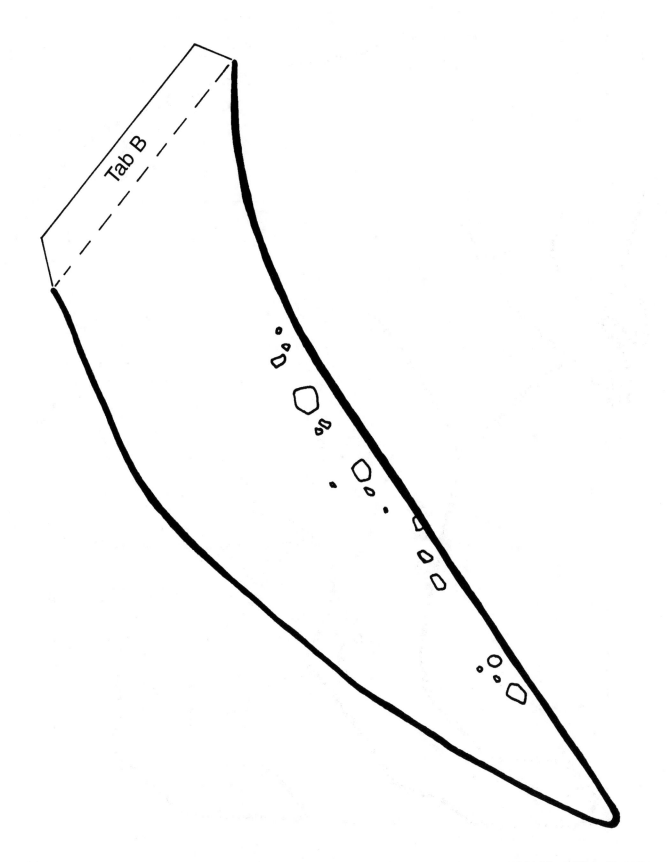

Triceratops

Use pages 368–370. Attach the head to the torso at Tab A. Attach the tail to the torso at Tab B.

Triceratops (cont.)

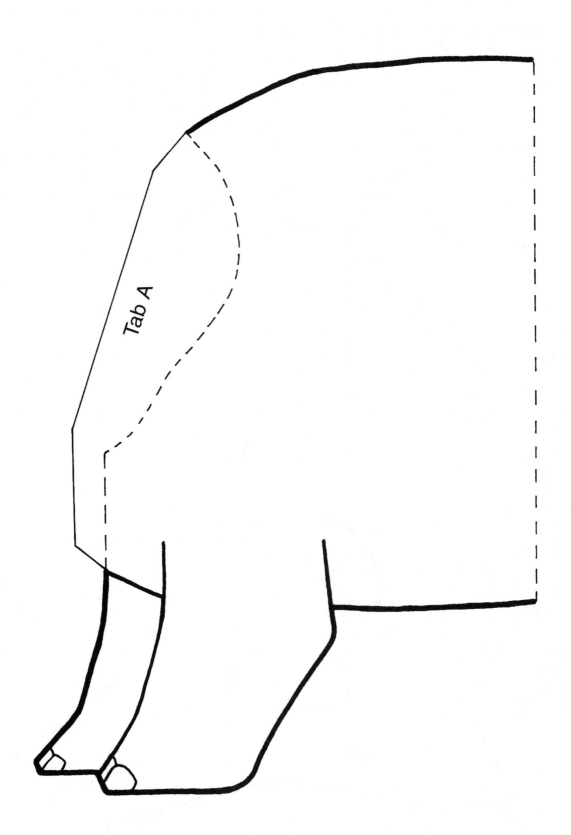

Tab A

Triceratops *(cont.)*

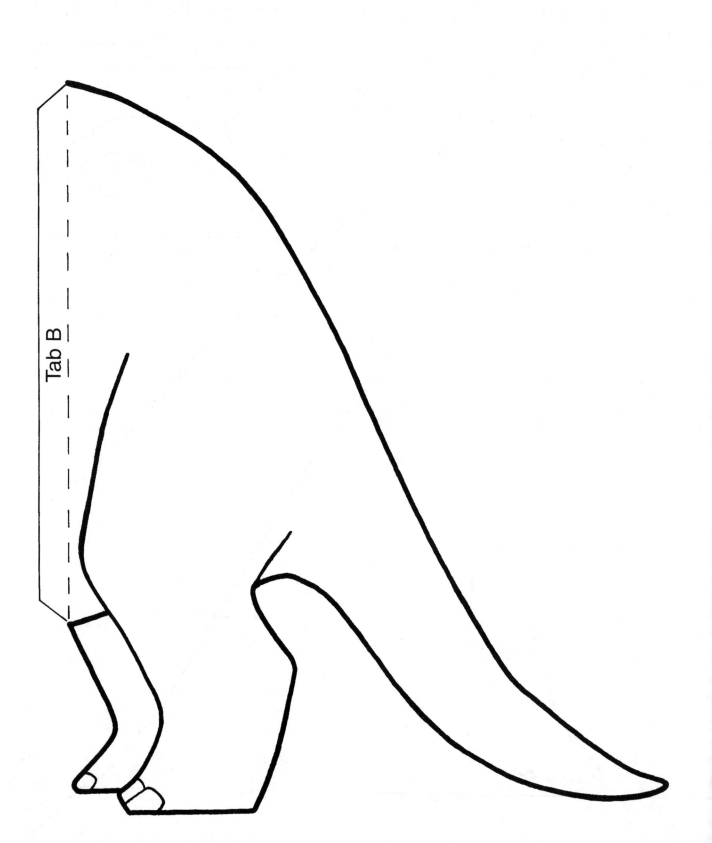

Tab B

370

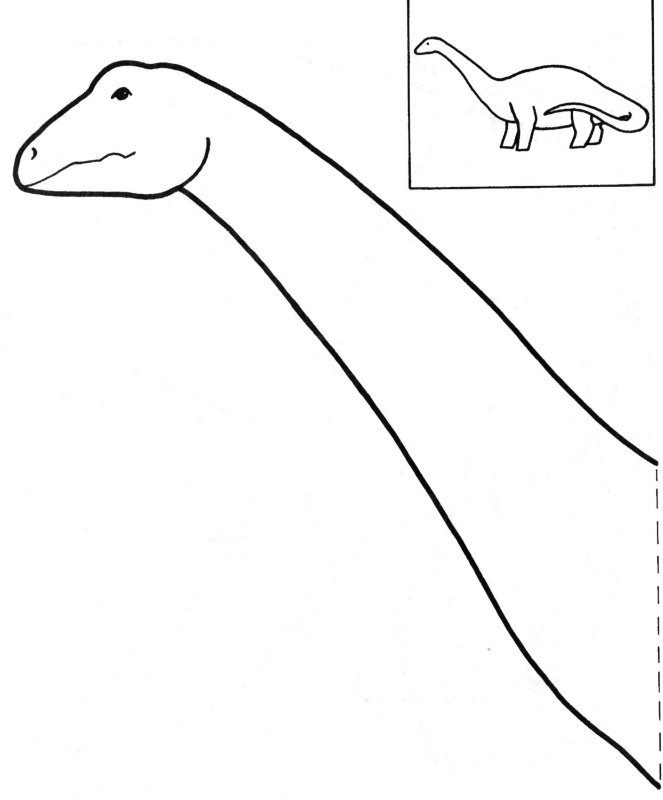

Apatosaurus

Use pages 371–373. Attach the head to the torso at Tab A. Attach the tail to the torso at Tab B.

© Teacher Created Materials, Inc.   371   #3801 Big & Easy Patterns

Apatosaurus *(cont.)*

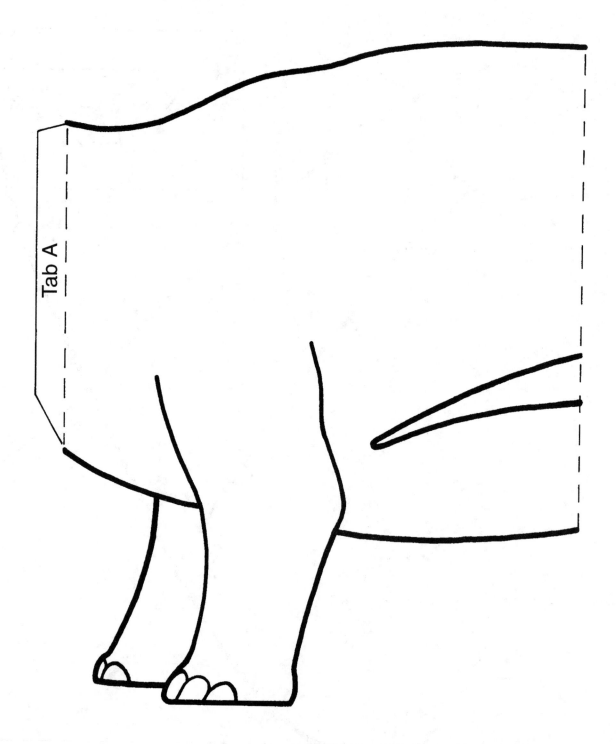

Apatosaurus *(cont.)*

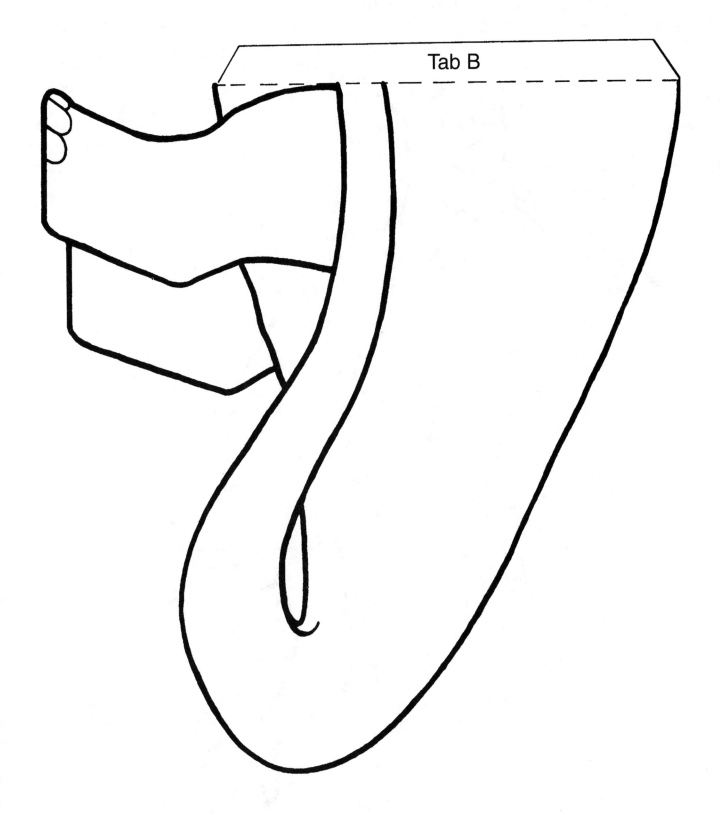

Tab B

Pteranodon

Use pages 374–375. Attach the left wing to the torso at Tab A. Attach the right wing to the torso at Tab B.

Pteranodon *(cont.)*

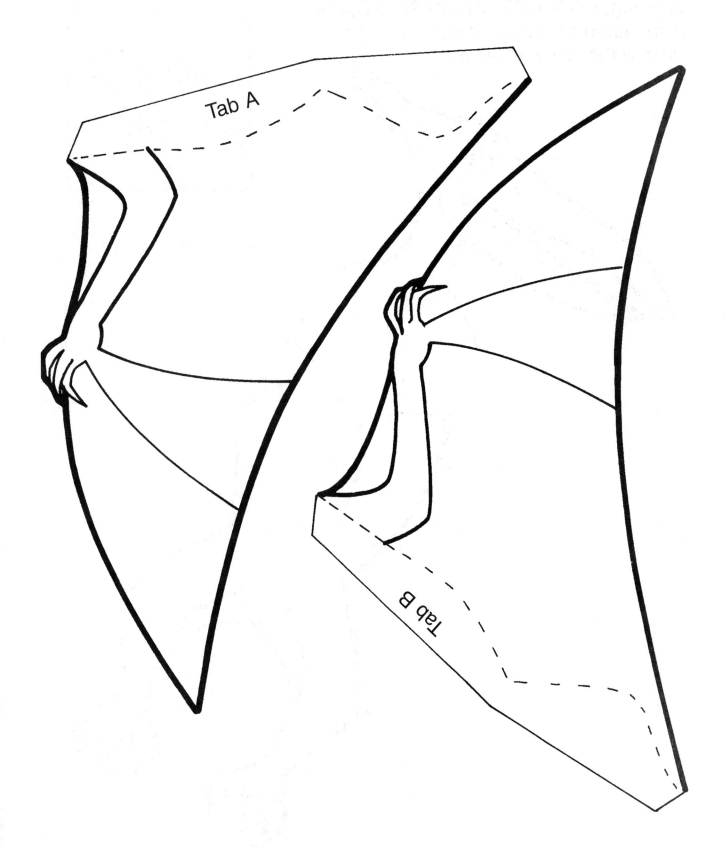

Tab A

Tab B

Stegosaurus

Use pages 376–378. Attach the head to the torso at Tab A. Attach the tail to the torso at Tab B.

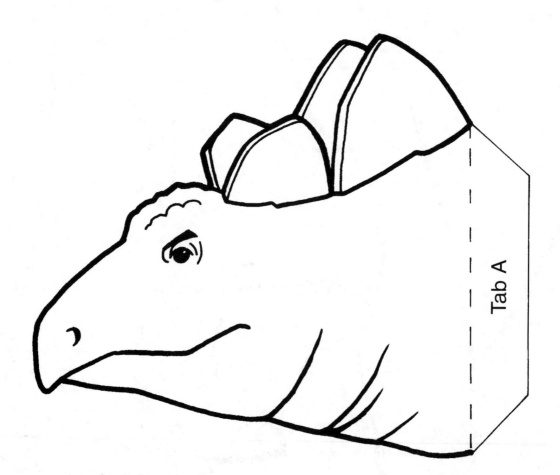

Tab A

Stegosaurus *(cont.)*

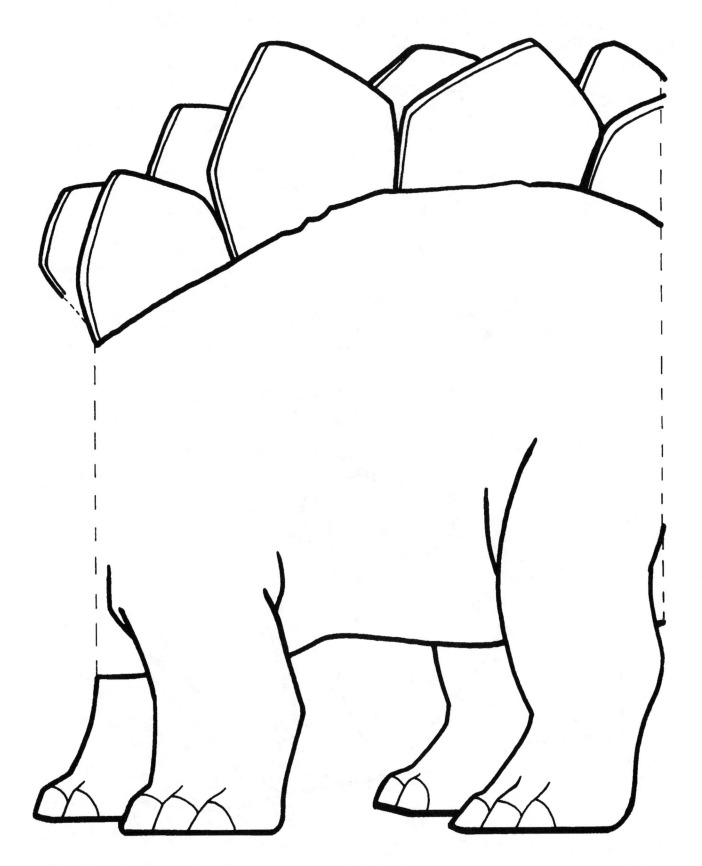

Stegosaurus (cont.)

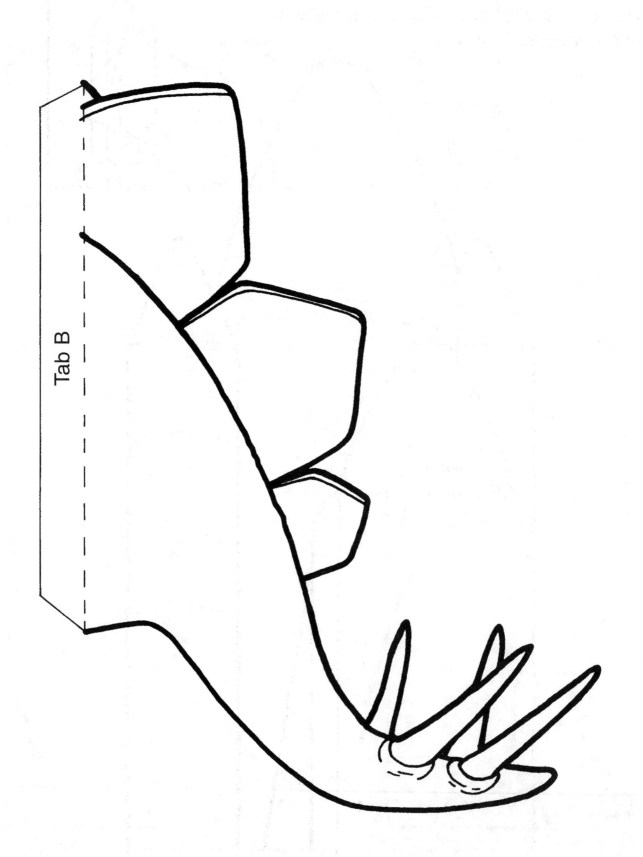

Tab B

Space Shuttle

Use pages 379–380. Cut out the shuttle and connect at the tab.

Space Shuttle *(cont.)*

Tab

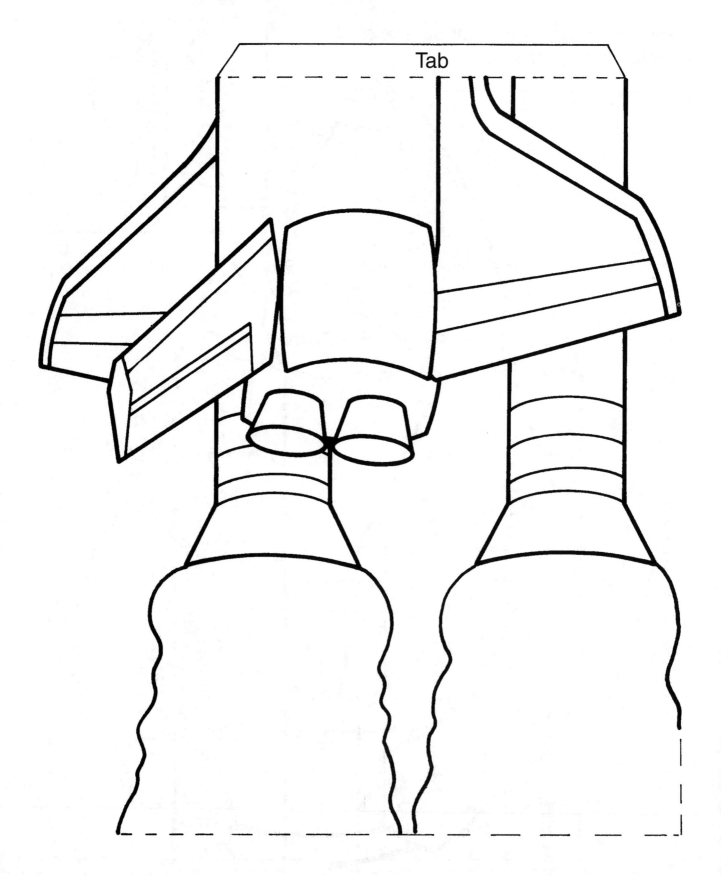

380

Astronaut

Use pages 381–382. Cut out and connect at the tab.

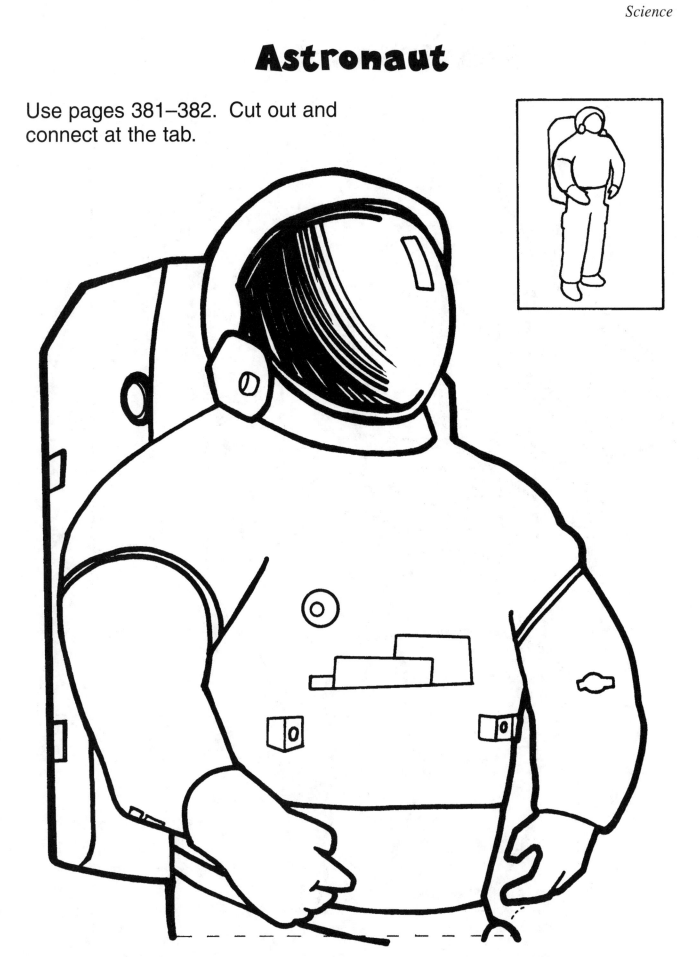

Astronaut *(cont.)*

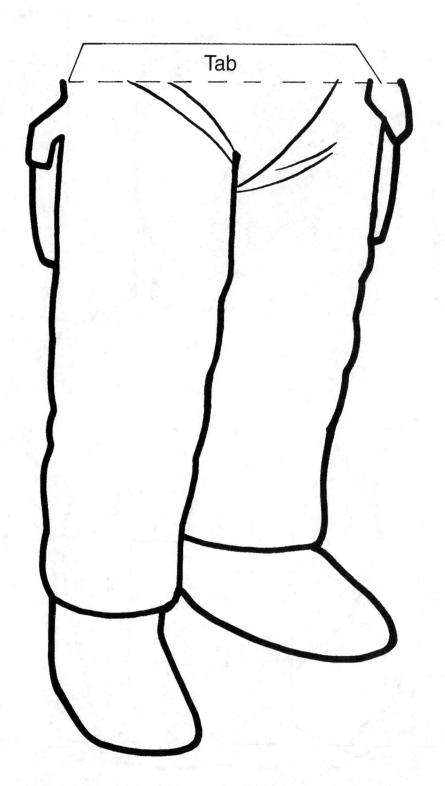

Tab

382

Recycling

Use pages 383–385.

Newspapers

Cardboard

Milk Jug

Soda Bottle

Recycling *(cont.)*

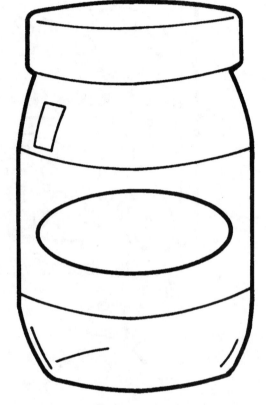

Glass Jar

Soda Can

384

Recycling Labels

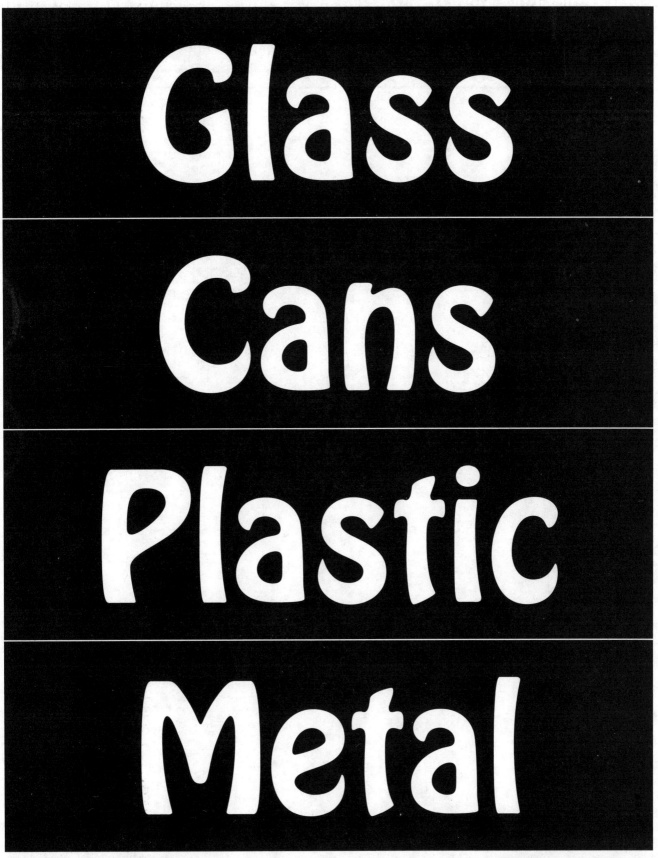

Lunch Box

Use pages 386–388. Make two lunch boxes per student. Cut out the lunch boxes and tape them together at the bottom.

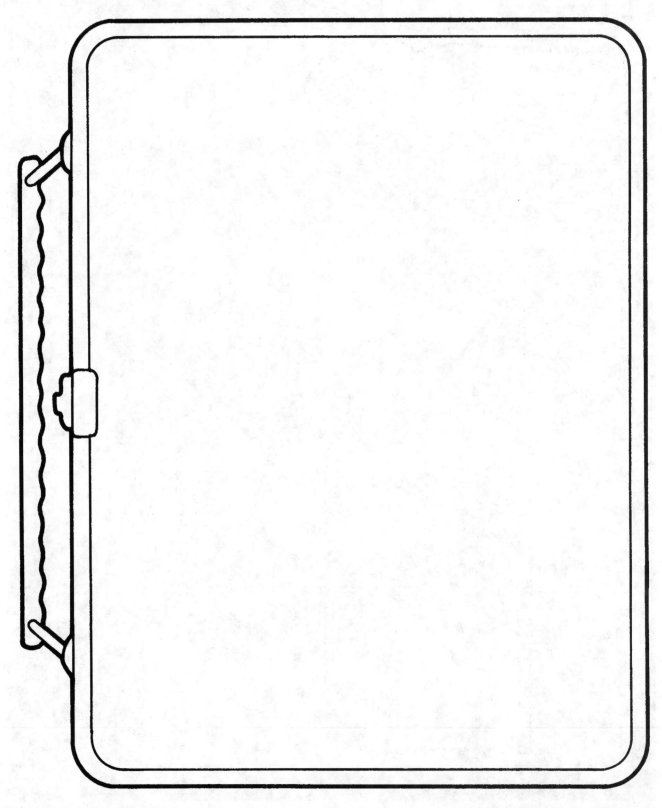

386

Snacks

Copy pages 387–388 for each student to use with the lunch box on page 386.

Snacks (cont.)

Copy pages 387–388 for each student to use with the lunch box on page 386.

Food Pyramid

Use pages 389–390. Cut out and connect at the tab.

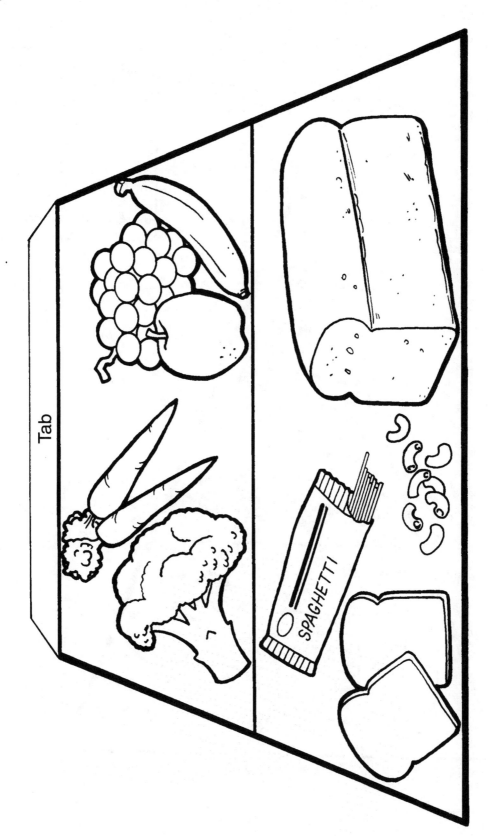

Food Pyramid *(cont.)*

Tooth

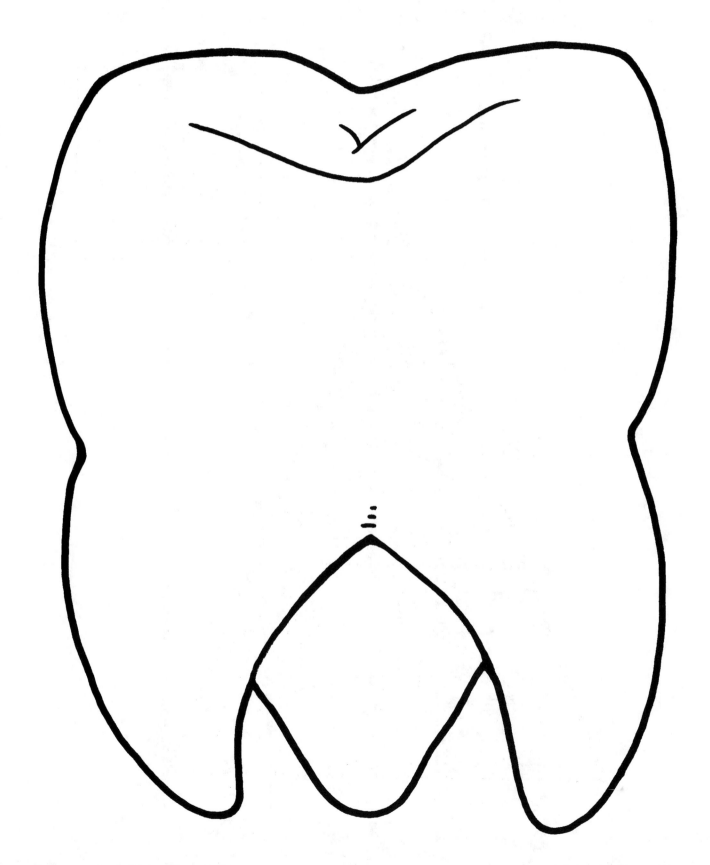

Toothbrush

Cut out and connect at the tab.

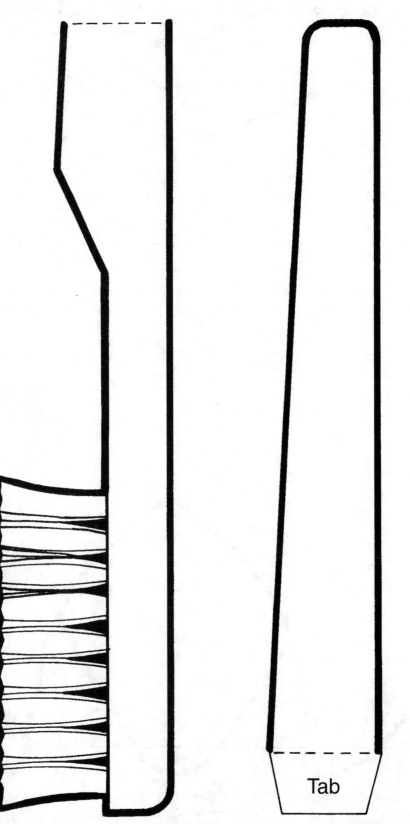

Tab

Toothpaste

Cut out and connect at the tab.

BUBBLES

TOOTHPASTE

Tab

Five Senses

Ear

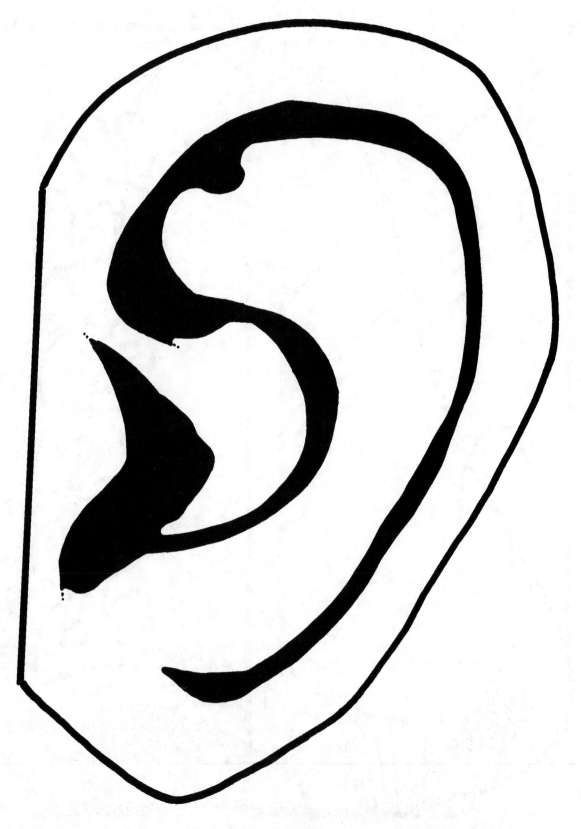

Five Senses *(cont.)*

Nose

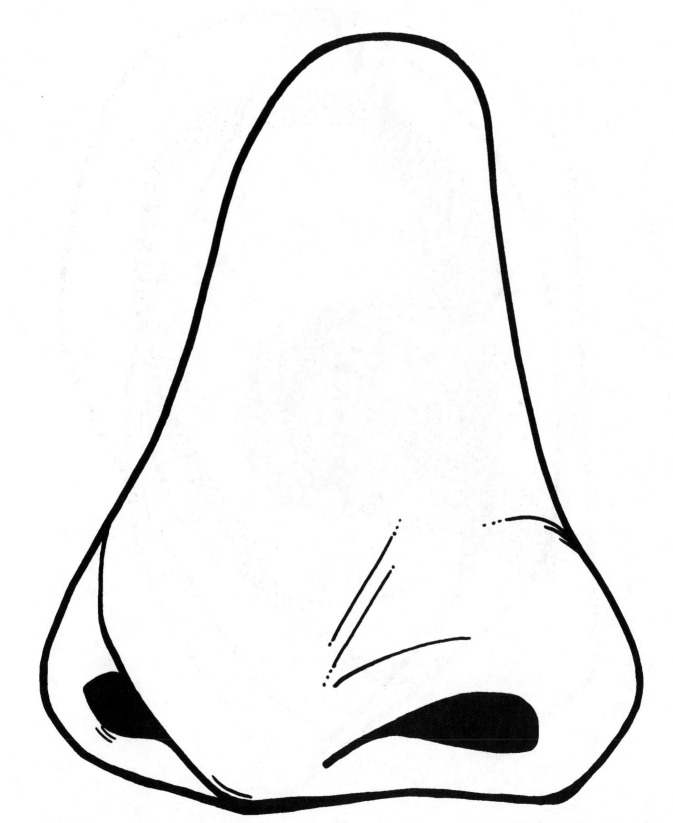

Five Senses (cont.)

Eye

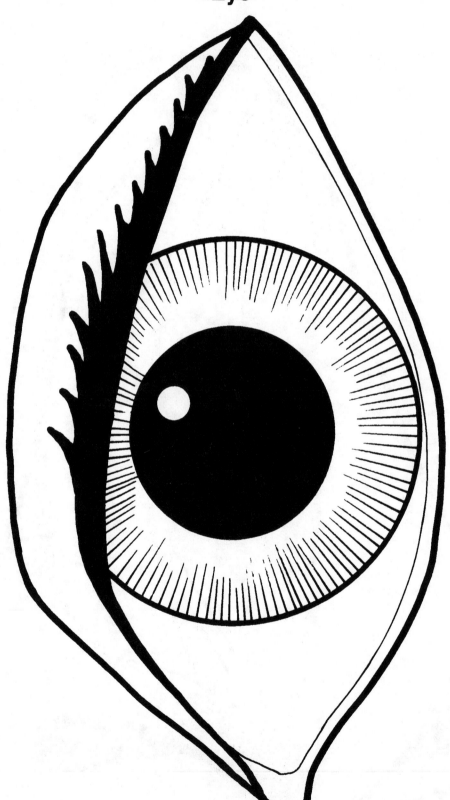

396

Five Senses (cont.)

Mouth

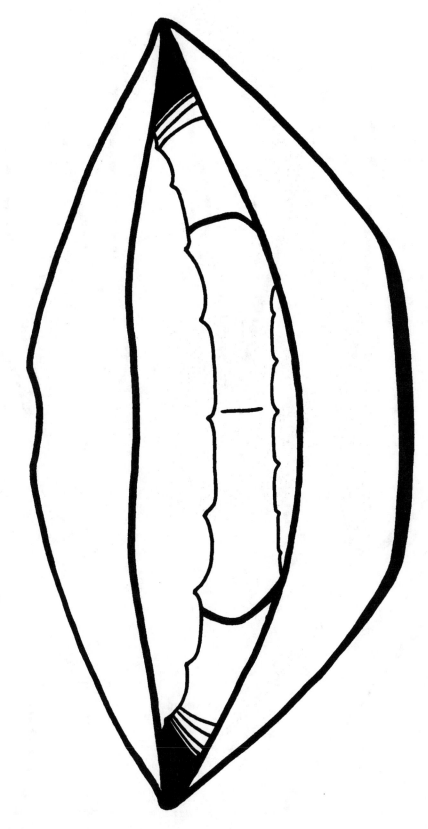

Five Senses *(cont.)*

Hand

Analog Clock

Use pages 399–400. For best results, use heavy paper and laminate the assembled clock and hands. Attach the hands using a paper fastener or brad to allow movement.

Analog Clock *(cont.)*

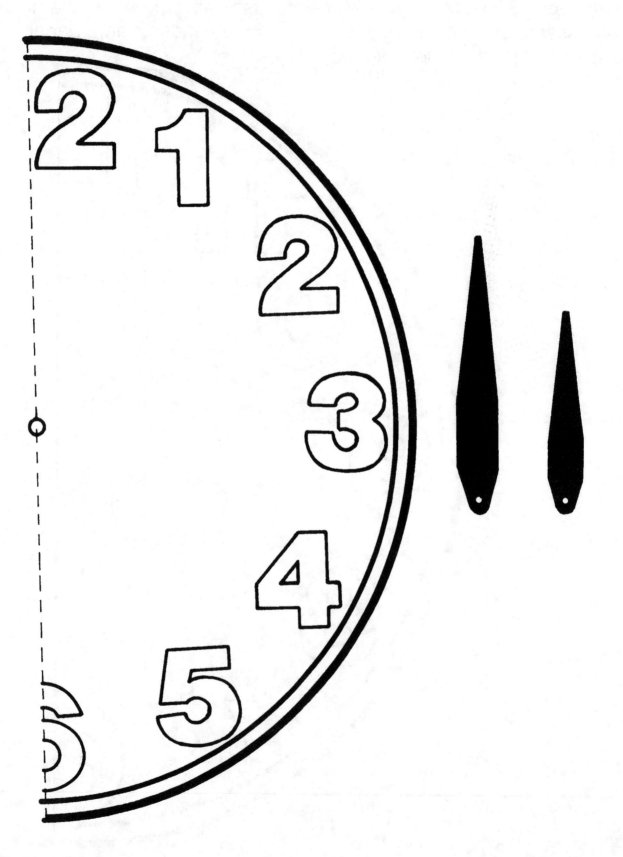

Pizza Fractions

Use pages 419–420.

Cut out and connect at the tab.

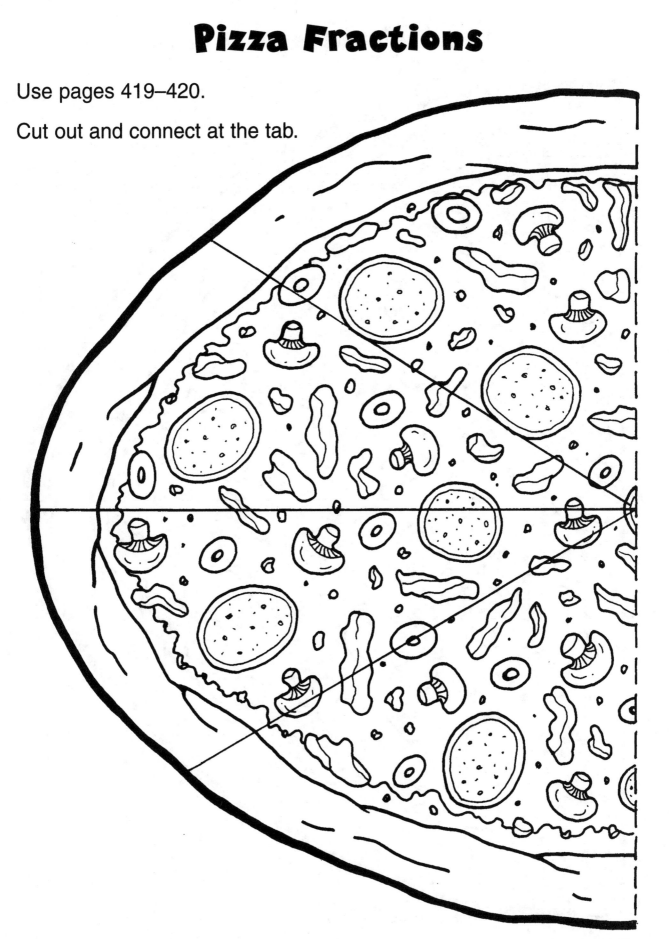

Pizza Fractions *(cont.)*

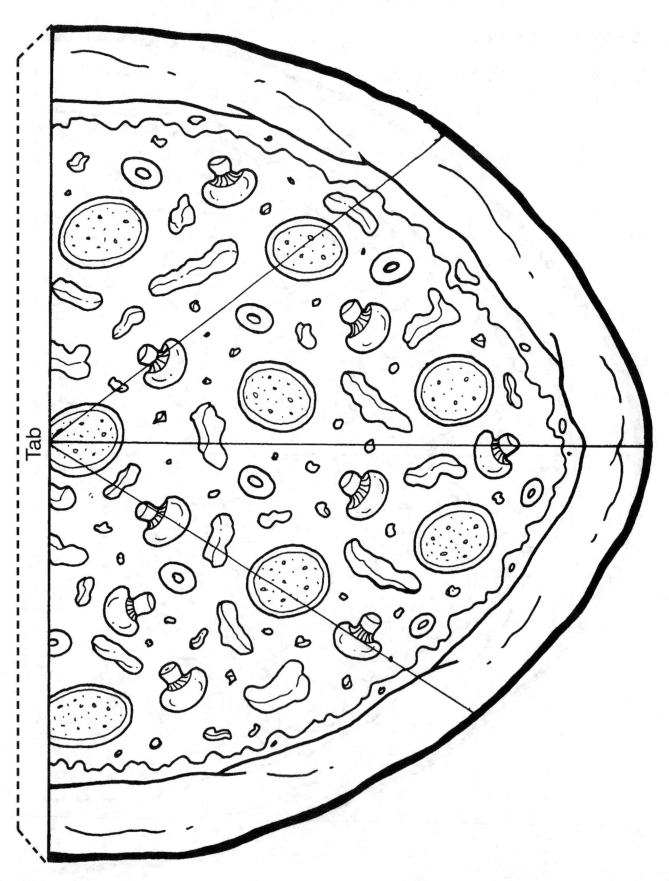

Tab

420

Apple Fractions

Use pages 421–422.

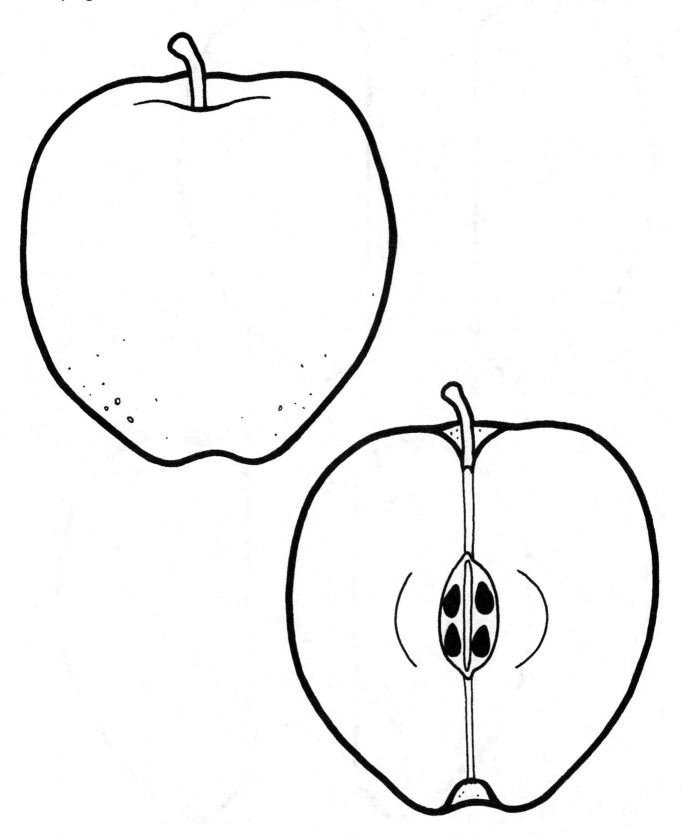

Apple Fractions *(cont.)*

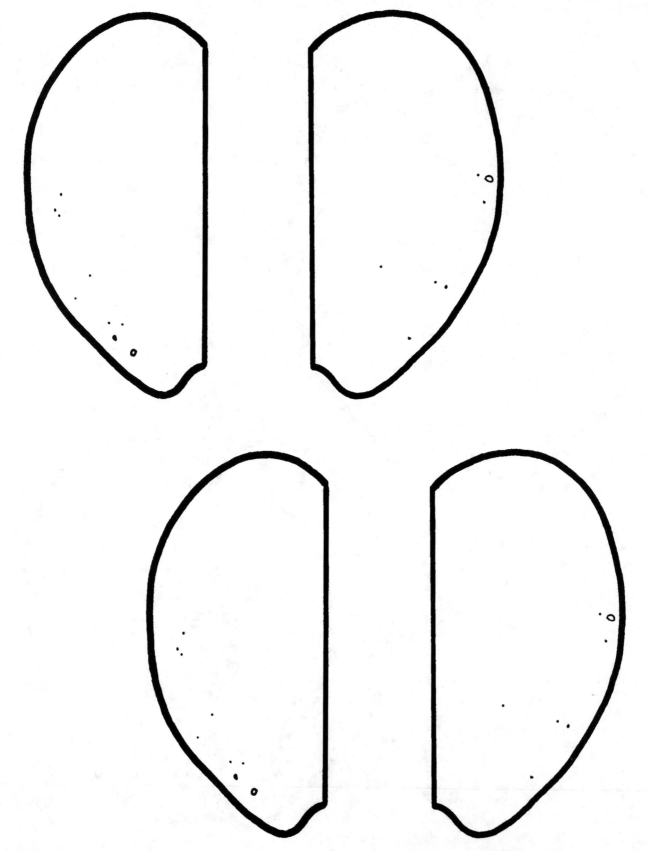

Pie Fractions

Use pages 423–424. Cut out and connect at the tab.

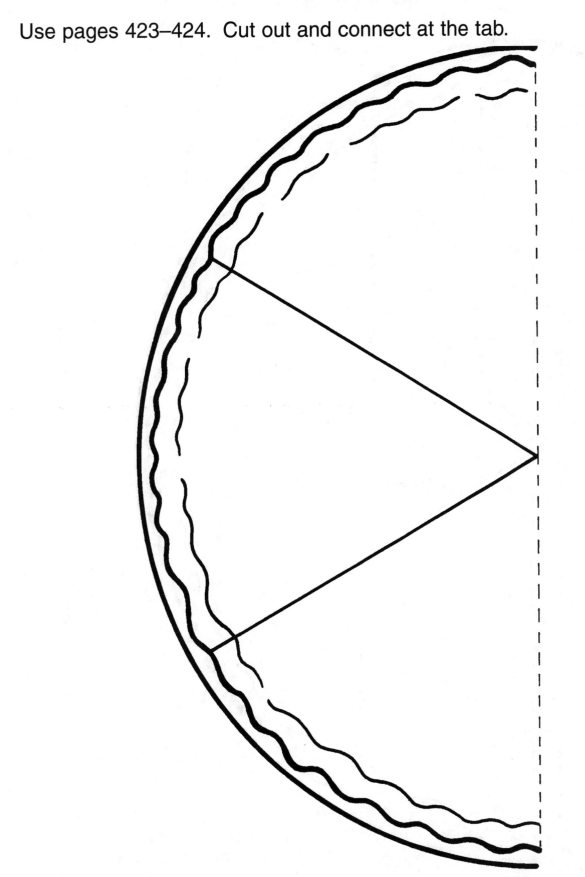

Pie Fractions *(cont.)*

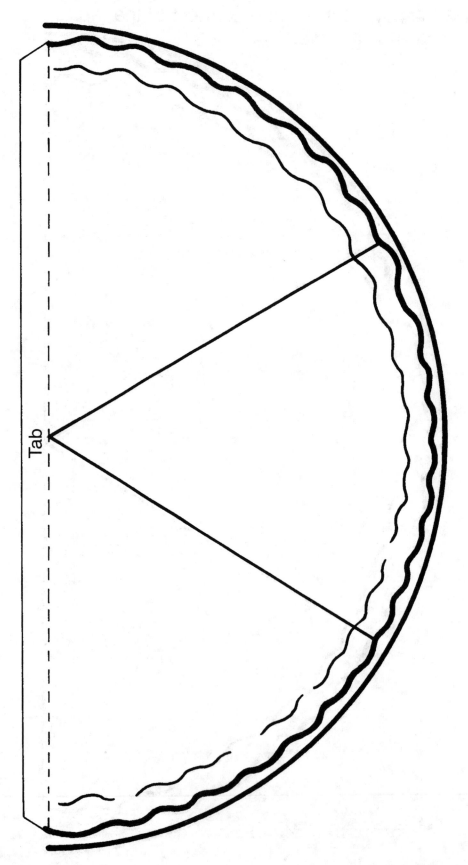

Tab

Candy Bar Fractions

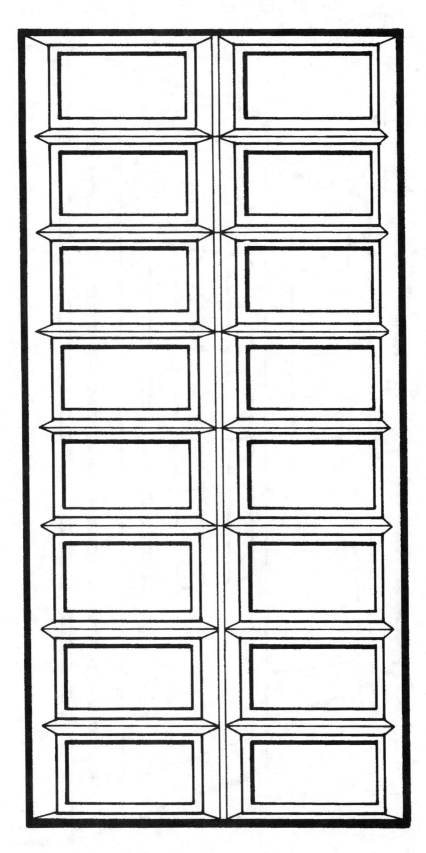

Cash Register

Use pages 426–427. Add appropriate numbers.

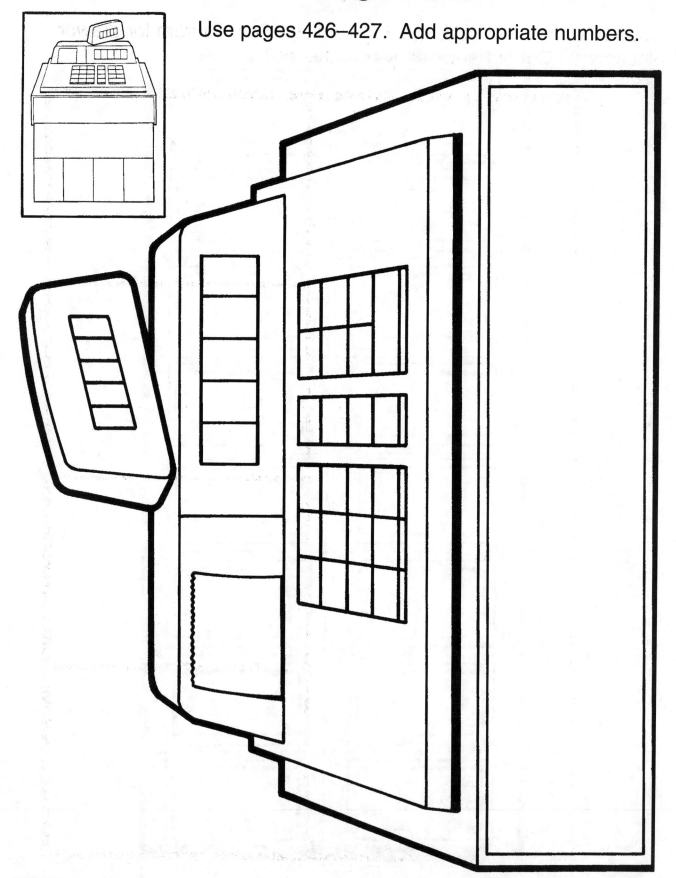

426

Cash Register *(cont.)*

Label drawers with monies being studied. See diagram for drawer placement. Cut out and connect at the tab.

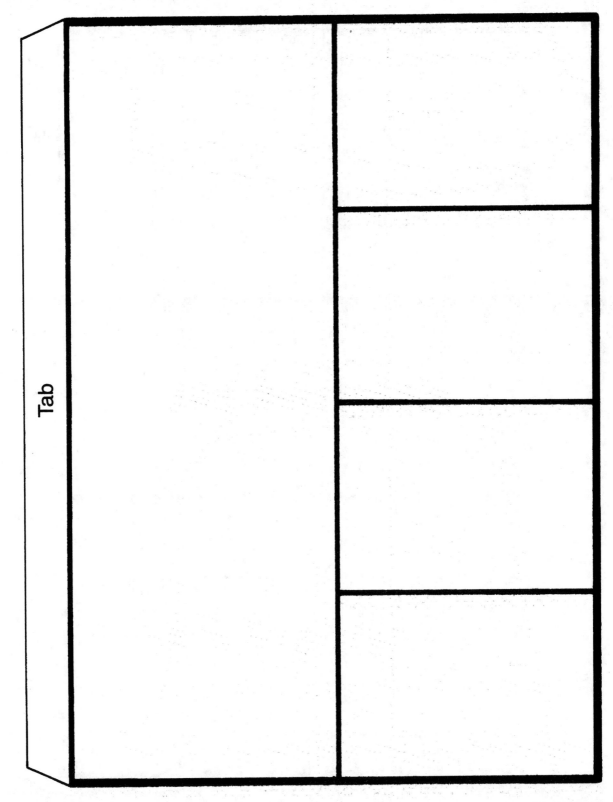

Ruler

Cut out and connect Tabs A and B.

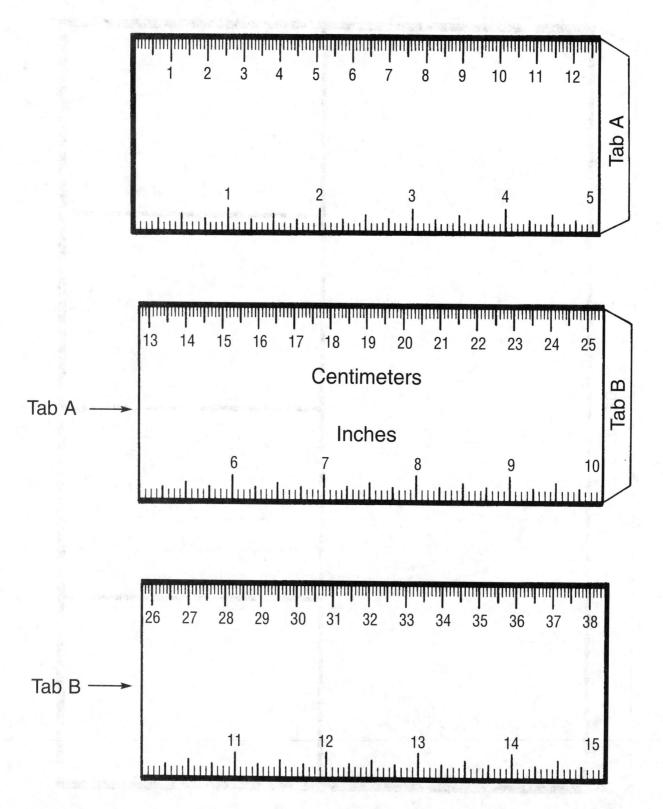

428

Tape Measure

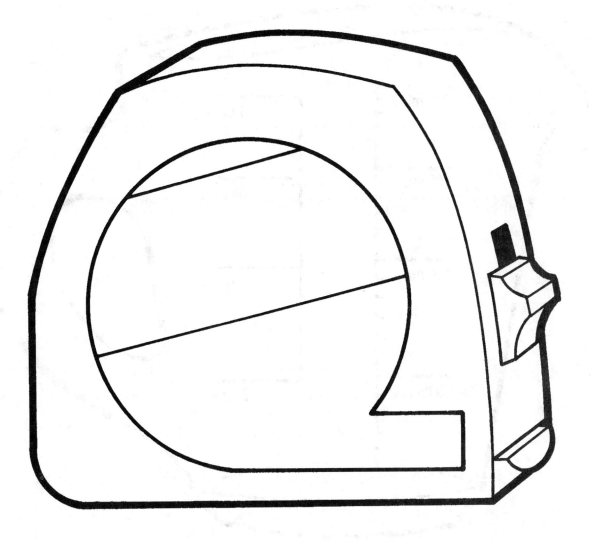

Measuring Cup

240 mL

180 mL

120 mL

60 mL

8 oz.

6 oz.

4 oz.

2 oz.

Pints and Quarts

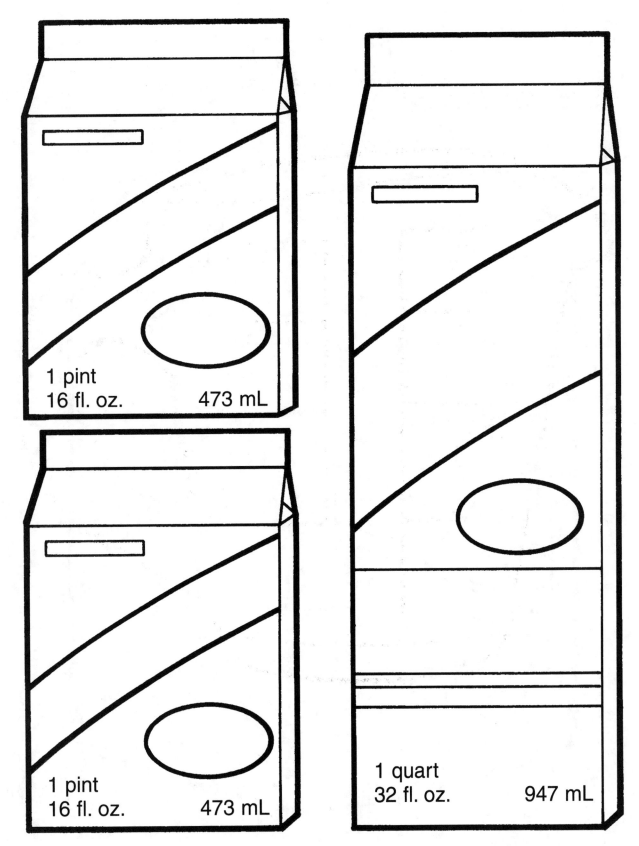

1 pint
16 fl. oz.   473 mL

1 pint
16 fl. oz.   473 mL

1 quart
32 fl. oz.   947 mL

 #3801 Big & Easy Patterns

Gallon

1 gal.
3.78 L